W9-BNH-340

YOU AND YOUR AGING PARENTS

YOU AND YOUR AGING PARENTS

by Edith M. Stern

with Mabel Ross, M.D.

HARPER & ROW, *Publishers*

NEW YORK AND EVANSTON

AUTHORS' NOTE

Although every story in this book is based on real-life instance, all proper names are fictitious.

FIRST EDITION

LIBRARY OF CONGRESS CATALOG CARD NUMBER: 65-14676

C–P

"Everywhere the human cycle begins with the dependency of the young on those who are older, and usually ends with the dependency of the very old on those who are younger."

Leo W. Simmons, Ph.D.

CONTENTS

ACKNOWLEDGMENTS

In connection with this new, revised, and enlarged edition, we acknowledge with gratitude the invaluable help of Dr. Clark Tibbitts, tireless pioneer and authority in gerontology, deputy director, Office of Aging, Department of Health, Education and Welfare, Washington, D.C., who reviewed our manuscript; and of William A. Stern, II, attorney, Miami, Florida, who supplied legal and financial data.

We are still indebted, in connection with the first edition, to Dr. Robert H. Felix, then director of the National Institute of Mental Health; Miss Flora Fox, then director of the Central Bureau for the Jewish Aged, New York City; and Dr. Leo W. Simmons, then professor of sociology at Yale University, who reviewed our script. We are especially indebted to the late Miss Rose J. McHugh, then chief of the Welfare Service Standards Branch, Bureau of Public Assistance, Federal Security Agency, who not only acted as a reviewer but also brought us together as collaborators, thereby instituting a deep friendship which has miraculously survived two grueling collaborations.

The Authors

PART I

In The Course of Human Events...

1

YOUR NEW JOB

When your parents are aging, if their health and strength are failing, or they don't have enough money to cover their living expenses, or if one of them has died and the other is left all alone, it is the most natural thing in the world for you to be troubled. Of course you were always vaguely aware of the fact that some day, instead of your being able to turn to them, they would have to turn to you. Nevertheless, the first time you are asked, "Son, what do you think we ought to do?"; the first time you ask yourself, "How can they get along best?" is bound to be disturbing.

Not only does it come hard to think of your parents as growing old, and no longer able to manage entirely for themselves, but also you feel torn. Though you want to do everything humanly possible for their comfort and happiness, you'd like to keep disruption of your own life to a minimum.

If you have been living alone, whether you are presently working, or retired, or have never worked, you have your own established pattern of daily life. If you are married, the family you have founded is what sociologists call a "nuclear family"; that is, the definite unit consisting of father, mother, and their offspring. At any stage of your nuclear family life, during any phase of your own, a new responsibility for your parents is disturbing.

If you have young children, they need your time and attention. If you have teenagers you are involved emotionally with their problems and financially with their education. After the last child has left home, you and your husband or wife want to feel free to enjoy each other's companionship: a man may just be beginning to enjoy financial security, and a woman, after many years of housewifery, to take up a work life or career on her own.

A little later, say in the fifties—although age-based problems are relative, depending on the individual—you may have some of the kind of worries which are not uncommon in middle life, such as if you lost your job would you be able to get another? Or, if you have been upped by your company or agency, you may have heavier, more complex, lonelier responsibilities than ever before.

New in civilization, and insofar as we know to a large extent new even since the first edition of this book, is the number of Americans, themselves sixty or over, who have quite aged parents; and as longevity increases so will the proportion increase. Just at the time, therefore, when your own well-earned retirement is imminent or already a fact, you may have a particularly harassing, unprecedented job: the care of an aged parent in the eighties, nineties, or possibly even older.

At any stage, to complicate matters further, you are probably short of space, or money, or both. You tell yourself that you ought not to mind caring for your parents in their old age, because they did so much for you, and that any reluctance to welcome them with open arms into your life or home is outrageously ungrateful. You run over in your mind all your friends and acquaintances who seem cheerfully to take in their old folks, and you are convinced that something is wrong with you even to think of Mother's or Father's care as a burden. You feel that you should want to have your parents with you, and you torment yourself with all kinds of self-accusations because really you don't.

Perhaps you consider your problem exceptional, but actually you are in plenty of company. There are some 18 million men and women over sixty-five in our population, about 12,000 of them more than one hundred years old. According to the 1960 census, 2,400,000 households are three-generational, and over 39,000 four-generational!

If you could live inside most homes harboring two or more grown generations you would discover that no matter how well, to an outsider, everyone seemed to be getting along, not everything was sweetness and light. One educated guess is that only about half of such households really work out smoothly. A "good" son or daughter whom you'd like to emulate may actually be making life pretty miserable for parents, and what is all amiability in public might be superciliousness or harshness in private. As for those delightful old people about whom you read in the newspapers and whom you wish your parents resembled—well, you'd probably be able to find out what they're like to live with only from their sons or daughters. Quite possibly these grand old men and women are not as wise and understanding and open-minded and tolerant about the little events of daily life as they are about politics, science, art, or how they have managed to live so long, nor might they be nearly as fascinating to children with whom they live as they are to reporters.

The dear little old lady and beaming old gentleman of fiction are rarities in real life. Old folks are people, with all other people's crochets and faults, plus some intensified by age and lack of intelligent preparation for it, while their adult children are not angels either but also people who, like yourself, have habits and ideas they don't relish modifying.

Nor, you may be sure, are the older people thoroughly happy about the situation. They think they ought to be glad to be living with their children and are distressed when they're not. Most don't like losing their independence and becoming their children's children. Most like to be in contact with their children, to be sure, and to live nearby, but in their own homes. Most feel that they ought to be grateful for being taken in and yet, uncomfortably, they can't seem to manage to be grateful. Over and over, during the course of their long lives, they have heard people saying about the childless, "Poor things, when they're old, they won't have a soul to take care of them," and they had more or less expected the sons or daughters they reared to help them out.

A great deal of nonsense has been talked and written about the decline of family life and modern disrespect of the young for their elders. But there is no evidence that feelings between grown children and their aging parents are significantly different from what they ever were. The very frequency of admonitions to honor the aged in old manuscripts suggests that respect for old people was not as deeply ingrained as was wished. Several studies have shown that nineteenth century American homes housing several generations, often nostalgically referred to as typical, were no more prevalent in proportion to the population than such homes today.

Indeed, for all the current wails and laments, "Honor thy Father and thy Mother" still has a deep, strong hold on all of us! Yet, despite the fact that the obligation of children to care for their aging parents is so firmly embedded in our morals and customs; despite the fact that the phase of life when it must be carried into action comes normally to everyone except orphans, often the necessity of having to "take Mother in" or "support Father" is met as if it were as untoward and accidental as a severe illness.

To some extent this is because of our national accent on youth, which is almost as unrealistic as the phrase, "married and lived happily ever after," neatly capping fairy tales. Our TV and movie culture, our popular fiction, even the family-living courses that prepare young folks for marriage and parenthood tend to ignore the fact that living may continue for decades even after middle age is reached, and that there is a point when concepts of "family life" must be revised to include the aged. The facts of life are more than the processes of reproduction. It is equally a fact of life that in the course of time the roles of parents and children become reversed, and the younger must take care of the elder.

When this happens, new adjustments are inevitable. Many are unwelcome and some unpleasant, but they are as much a normal part of living as those which grow out of any other major shift in individual or family circumstances. For instance, when two adults marry, neither can go on precisely as before, and either may have to give up anything from a cherished freedom to stay out all night to a preference as to how far the windows should be open. When gay young couples begin to rear families and must care for small children, this affects their time, their budgets, their habits of recreation, and, indeed, nearly everything else in their previous way of life.

Similarly, when anyone goes to work a host of adjustments are necessary. As a matter of fact, your new responsibility for your aging parents is very much like a new job. As in all jobs, it brings with it restrictions on your coming and going where you please and doing what you please when you please. It involves an interplay of personalities, with everyone having to make some concessions in order to get along with others. Money, as in every job, plays its part.

Along with frustrations there can also be some very real satisfactions and rewards.

But above all it is a job to be faced as challenging for your heart and mind, one to be undertaken with reflection and analysis of yourself, your parent, and the family situation as a whole. Perhaps with plain common sense, or perhaps with prayer and meditation, you will be able to answer satisfactorily, "What can I do?" But then again perhaps you will need professional help from a counselor to clarify the situation, the problems in it, and their solution. In any case, it is a job that has to be done, and the more thoughtfully and feelingly you do it the more successful it will be.

It may be that the aging person with whom you are concerned is a grandparent, or an aunt or uncle who brought you up, or one who has no children or other younger relatives to whom to turn. In that case, your sense of responsibility and your reactions are likely to be quite similar to those you would have toward a parent. Although throughout this book we shall say "parents" or "mother" or "father" as a matter of simplification and convenience, you can assume that nearly everything we discuss applies to any aging relatives to whom you stand in the place of a child. Indeed, the older man or woman who looks to you for guidance or a home may not even be a blood relative, but someone like a nurse or governess or housekeeper who, after long years of service, may have become almost one of the family.

In this book, we are going to point out and suggest how you can do your job with the least possible annoyance and irritation and the greatest possible amount of contentment and happiness for all concerned.

2

YOU CONSIDER PLANS FOR LIVING ARRANGEMENTS

When you begin to think over all the possible living arrangements that might be made for your parents, you will probably find that each has its drawbacks. If they stay where they are, alone in their own home, you fear that you will be continually worried about them. What's more, you will never know when you might have to pick up and visit them to tide them through minor illnesses or bad weather or any circumstances with which they can't cope. They might, of course, remain in their own home with someone engaged to look after them, but you see two catches in this. Would the person you engaged be dependable? Would the cost be prohibitive?

Also, they might move to one of the apartment houses especially designed for the elderly, or to a retirement community or to a retirement hotel. But if none of these facilities is nearby, you might feel almost as worried about their "being so far away" as if they stayed where they are.

Now of course you and your family might move in to your parents' home, if it's large enough. Or they might move in with you. But you certainly have reservations about either of these steps, bound to upset your present way of life.

There is one other possible move. Your parents might be turned over to someone else's care: in a boarding home, in an old people's home with a capital *H,* in a nursing home, or in a hospital. But you recoil from this idea. You think of *King Lear*. You think of what the neighbors would say. You think about the time your mother didn't leave the house for six weeks to nurse you through an illness, and about how much your father sacrificed to send you through school. The last thing you want to do is to treat Mother and Father as if you were discarding them.

But something has to be done. You and they must come to a decision on some plan. And you will save yourself a great deal of wear and tear if you base it primarily not on what you would like to do or even what you should do, but what you can do. Maybe this sounds like a pretty obvious piece of advice. There are, however, sons and daughters beating their brain out against facts which inexorably frustrate good intentions and wishful, loving plans.

One of them, for instance, was Leo Hunt, whose eighty-two-year-old mother refused to budge from the eight-room apartment where she had lived for forty years. Mr. Hunt's wife was an invalid, so he could not take his mother into his own home, but he wanted her to board with a congenial family instead of staying by herself. He begged, he entreated, he pleaded, but the old lady was adamant; she was going to stay right where she was, she declared, until they carried her out feet first. Mr. Hunt would wake up during the night and break into a cold sweat as he thought about what would happen if his mother were trapped in a fire or fell down and broke her leg or fainted, and he worried himself into such a state of ill health that he became almost as much of an invalid as his wife. And to no end; Mother kept on living alone.

You can avoid undergoing fruitless agonies like Leo Hunt's if, after a reasonable attempt at persuasion, you proceed to accept the inevitable. Ask yourself, right at the beginning of your new job, "How much will they let me do? Will they allow me to run their lives? Will they consent to selling their home or moving?" Then, if you find them determined to stay put, make up your mind there is nothing to do but let them. By trying to engineer a move, you have done all that you can, and you have no negligence with which to reproach yourself. After all, adults, however elderly, are not babies who can be picked up bodily and carried where you wish.

The next point to settle for yourself is "How much are they able to do for themselves?" If they are completely helpless, of course staying by themselves is out of the question, and in this case they can, might, and probably will want to be carried out. Very likely the possibility of your living together also will be eliminated if they are bedridden and require constant nursing care.

Now consider what you and they can afford. If it is very little, a nurse-housekeeper is out, and the state of your finances will also influence the boarding-with-a-family or nursing-home ideas. If you cannot raise enough money between you to keep two households going, half your decision is already made. Without question, you will have to double up.

Next, review the possibilities of where and how. It might be desirable for all of you to move to a house or apartment better arranged for two families than the one in which either lives now, but if you cannot find one for your price you may have to give up this idea temporarily. There remains the option of your present home or that of your parents. If yours consists of one room or the old folks refuse to move, this decision, too, is out of your hands.

Another bar to your preferences may be what you are personally able to do for your parents. What is the state of your health? Are you employed during the day? If you are not well enough to take on any new responsibilities, or if you have to be out of the house when your parents need to be given their meals or require other kinds of attention, you may not be able to give them the kind of care they need. In that case you cannot consider living together.

If, through an unfortunate combination of circumstances, "It can't be done" applies to every one of the living arrangements we have mentioned, consult a privately or publicly supported family service agency, if one exists in or near your community. Perhaps your church or the diocese or synod to which it belongs has a family service and counseling agency. Or the Community Chest may support one that is non-sectarian. Inquire at the Council of Social Agencies in your community (which may be called the Welfare Planning Council, Community Council, Family Services, or by some other name.) If you look in the classified telephone directory under "Agencies" you will track down other sources of information. The Family Service Association of America, 44 East 23rd Street, New York, 10010, New York will tell you which family service agency is nearest you.

The chances are, however, that even after you have systematically eliminated the impossibilities, some choice of possibilities will remain as to whether you will live together or apart. Just as you considered the practicalities in determining which course to take, now consider the more subtle and complex matter of the personalities involved, for the "right" and "wrong" of your decision is dependent on these rather than on any set arrangements. What is right for one family may be all wrong for another. Think of the situation as if you had a choice of two highways leading to the same place. Neither is the right road, neither the wrong one; you select whichever better suits your particular purpose.

Likewise, it may be good for an old person to be part of one household, and bad to be part of another. The Clark family is an example of one where it was right for Mr. Clark's mother to move in. The younger Mrs. Clark's own mother had died when she was a small child, and she welcomed having an older woman near to love her and be loved. A rather dependent person, she disliked being alone and was delighted to have company in the house while her husband was at work and her children at school. Doing for her mother-in-law, who needed quite a good deal of physical care, made her feel useful, a deep satisfaction for any of us. Getting along with her—which the old lady's own daughter could not do—made her feel successful and competent. "They couldn't put up with her," the younger Mrs. Clark would say with a small superior smile.

The Waters' family situation, on the other hand, demonstrates that sometimes it is equally right for Mother *not* to move in, though it took Mrs. Waters a long time and an almost constant hell of guilt feelings and self-reproach before she came to realize this. The Waters and their children had a cramped small house in a small town, but when Mrs. Waters' mother, Mrs. Glenn, who lived in a large city, was left widowed at sixty-five with almost no money, like a good daughter, Mrs. Waters felt that she certainly ought to ask Mother to live with them. Mr. Waters was unenthusiastic, though willing; and they deferred an outright invitation. Meanwhile, from time to time, Mrs. Glenn would visit, and each visit was less successful than the last. Mrs. Glenn, accustomed to a lively social life with lifelong friends, to window shopping, crowds of people, and all the excitement and bustle of metropolitan life, was bored to distraction by the birds and the bees and the flowers.

Mrs. Waters, irritated, wished to high heaven that her temperamentally gadabout mother, instead of constantly complaining about "the sticks" and "the quiet," would settle down and be grandmotherly, like other people's mothers, and once, just once, offer to baby-sit so she and Ralph could go out. Still, Mrs. Waters worried about how Mother was ever going to be able to get along, and felt that she was the worst of daughters not to convert the living room into a permanent refuge for Mrs. Glenn.

That was five years ago. Mrs. Glenn is still not living with the Waters, and the visits have grown farther and farther apart because she is having too good a time on her own to languish in what she considers "the country." Somehow or other she always manages to find ways of earning a few dollars, like listing herself for jury duty or doing part-time clerical work, that help to keep her going financially. She gives up her tiny furnished room in the winter and goes by bus to Florida and another furnished room. Her letters are gay with accounts of "Guess who I bumped into" and the men who take her to dinner. Definitely, it would be wrong for her to live with the Waters.

Although he is past eighty and somewhat feeble, so would it be wrong for Mr. Engelsman to move in with his son and daughter-in-law. He was one of those men who remain bachelors at heart no matter how long they have been married; he never did like having to come home on time for dinner, having cosmetics mixed in with his shaving things in the medicine closet, or having to watch his language and his jokes because women were present, and he certainly wasn't going to like domesticity with his daughter-in-law any more than with his wife. It was a wise move, therefore, and not "ditching the poor old man," as some of the Engelsman's friends said, when Mr. Engelsman, Jr., arranged for his father to move into a boarding home. Along with other old cronies he plays pinochle and poker in rooms thick with smoke, and he can enjoy endless man talk without "these women" interrupting. His relations with his son and daughter-in-law are completely affectionate. Every Wednesday night and Sunday when they call for him and take him to their house for dinner, he is glad to see them, happy to visit in their home, and happy to return again to his.

Mr. Sherman is an entirely different kind of person, so it is right that he live with his daughter. Simple in his tastes and needs, gentle and loving, he would have been shattered by the death of his wife when he was seventy-two, had he not been given his second chance to participate in family life. His particular contribution, according to him, is "taking the baby off her hands because she has so much to do," and every fine day the neighbors can see him taking his youngest grandchild out for a walk. It is a tossup whose face lights up the more, the toddler's or the grandfather's, when they look at each other; and "Throw the ball to Grandpa" or "Show Grandpa how you can run" are delightful routines for both.

Another pleasant home includes Mrs. Henry Chase, Sr. A year after her husband had died, when she was sixty-seven, she went to a social agency and said, "I have no one to look after now, my time is free, and I would like to do some volunteer work." Outgoing and attractive, she made an excellent "friendly visitor" to the homebound aged. Her son and daughter-in-law had most cordially invited her to live with them, but, she told the case worker who supervised her activities, "I don't want to be an 'interfering relative' and it's better that we live independently." When she was in her middle seventies, however, Mrs. Chase's eyes began to fail so seriously that it was not wise for her to drive, and she could not very well continue her volunteer activities. The social worker, concerned, suggested a conference with Henry Chase, Jr., and the upshot was that Mrs. Chase, Sr., consented to move in with him. Mrs. Chase, Jr., having had a good relationship with her mother-in-law for many years, and knowing that she moved in by necessity and not with the desire to run everybody and everything, is loving and kind. The children willingly read aloud now to Grandmother, who in the past had given them so much pleasure by reading aloud to them.

Beware, however, of your friends' notions—and usually well-meant, freely proffered advice—as to what is right or wrong for you to do about sharing a home with your parents. In all likelihood these will be based on set, generalized concepts of what is your duty, and to whom, rather than on the personality factors which they don't stop to consider, even were they in a position to know them. Also, bear in mind that much of what is said is based on sheer gossip, which can be very cruel; and that the sharpest criticisms of your not taking your parents into your home are liable to come from the individuals who would be the very last to take their own parents into their own homes, and must therefore let out their feelings of guilt on someone else.

Listen as politely as you can, and then proceed to custom-tailor your plans to the individuals whom you want to have them fit comfortably and well, always remembering that your decision needs to be based on more than whether you can all manage to get along together without too much quarreling. Your criterion should be something far more positive—the feasible happiness and contentment of members of at least two, or, if you have children, three generations.

Amiable dispositions, love, and individual personalities are not all that should come into the picture. Take into account, too, your parents' background and that of your own home. If they have lived all their lives on a farm and you live in a city apartment, will it really make them happy to be moved into surroundings where they must use unfamiliar devices like self-service elevators, get used to the squawks of taxi horns, and look out on brick walls instead of fields?

Or suppose they have lived in the same place all their lives, while yours is a military or corporation family which has to pick up and move every few years. Will they be more or less comfortable having to adjust periodically to new places and people than they would be staying put?

Would they be happy in your social setting? Miserable, for instance, was the retired college professor who moved in with his daughter and big-business-executive, country-club son-in-law. Accustomed to leading the quiet, contemplative existence of a scholar, with university teas the liveliest part of his social life, the sophisticated buffet dinners, the hilarious cocktail parties to which he was now exposed were disturbingly alien. If he retired to his room when his children had company, he felt ungracious; if he joined them, out of place. In any case, it was too noisy for him to go to sleep at his usual early bedtime, or he felt forlorn and lonely in the midst of dozens of people.

Finally, in making your plans for living arrangements, remember that this job may be a long one. Often sons and daughters, in the first flush of sympathy for a bereaved parent left a widower or widow, caught in a financial disaster, or newly invalided, invite their parents into their homes in a kind of spur-of-the-moment enthusiasm which loses sight of the family situation as a whole. It is one thing, for instance, to put up with crowding if Johnny will be leaving for college in a year or two or Mary is likely to get married soon, but another if Johnny and Mary are still in elementary school. It is one thing to give up temporarily the work you love or to refuse all social invitations because "Mother can't bear to be alone in the house," but quite another to make such sacrifices year after year.

In all tenderness, one of the greatest errors into which people fall when they take responsibility for their parents is thinking "It won't be for long" or "Mother and Father are pretty old, and I might as well do everything I can to make them happy for the few years they have left." Today especially, the evening of life is less likely to be short, like the tropical twilight brief between sunshine and darkness, than prolonged, like that of the temperate zone. The longer one lives, the better are the chances of living still longer. More individuals today are living more years than ever before, so "the short time that remains" may well stretch into years, even decades. The span of life between compulsory retirement and death can be longer than the periods between birth and marriage, or between marriage and the "empty nest." Therefore, the more you contemplate the care of your parents as something which requires the same careful consideration as anything else that involves long-term planning, the better your chances of making a go of the job.

This does not mean that at any specific moment you and your parents should agree to an ultimate plan. Take each necessary step only as it comes. Life is always in flux, but in the later years it is probably more difficult even to attempt to foresee what will happen than at any other time. An old person may be completely self sufficient today, and fall as many aged people do, and break his hip, and be dependent tomorrow. At over one hundred he may not have the slightest symptoms of senility, but at any time over sixty (and sometimes younger) senile brain disease may set in. A seventy-five-year-old may be hale, hearty, and robust, and then, in a relatively short time, be handicapped by impairment of sight or hearing. Under such circumstances, well-laid, well-working arrangements have to be scrapped.

Take Mrs. Strauss for instance. She became a widow at sixty-four and managed beautifully in a retirement hotel, financed by her children in a colder climate hundreds of miles away, until she was eighty. Indeed, on her eightieth birthday, she refused her daughter's invitation to celebrate in her home, "because my boy friend is going to take me out to a grand restaurant." The boy friend, aged eighty-two, died suddenly—a sad and shocking experience for Mrs. Strauss. Instead of refusing her daughter's invitations, no longer given, she begged to live with her—a quite unrealistic request, because the daughter had also become a widow, had to work, and now had neither space nor time to devote to her mother. Moreover, whether for emotional or physiological reasons, or both, for these are interrelated, Mrs. Strauss was becoming too forgetful and confused to live without constant supervision.

Then there is Miss Dodd, a distinguished professional woman, who until the age of seventy-nine maintained herself in luxurious independence in her own apartment, entertaining lavishly and remaining independent of an affectionate nephew and niece. But now after a succession of costly and debilitating illnesses, and the necessity of getting in a maid for the heavy housework and to prepare meals during convalescence, both she and they realize that new plans must be made.

It is also important to consider, especially if you yourself are beyond middle age, that it is your health which may break first. For the present, however—and think of it as only for the present—it might be the best plan for your mother, or father, or both, to continue living right in their own home.

PART II

You Live Apart

3

BUT THEY CAN'T LIVE ALONE—OR CAN THEY?

LONG BEFORE the facts warrant it, many a well-meaning son or daughter jumps to the conclusion that it is impossible for parents to manage by themselves. If you really want to do what is best for your parents, don't make this mistake. Loss of independence is a bitter pill to swallow, so the longer you can help your parents to enjoy the sweets of leading their own lives in their own way in their own place, the better.

If they and you can go on living for months or years as before, the advantages for your own household are obvious. But what may not be so obvious is the fact that this situation also has advantages for the aging. That a man's home is his castle holds as true at eighty-two as at twenty-eight, and when anyone must leave his castle something besides his body is liable to move out, too. The spirit of independence, of a sure place in the scheme of things, of being fully a person are as real a part of "my own home" as its bricks and mortar.

This is true of men as well as of women, popularly considered the only ones to whom "things around the house" mean much. Many men have a deep attachment for the lawns they developed from dirt and stones, the bookcases they built, the bushy shrubs they remember planting as mere twigs, or the particular armchair in the particular corner of the living room where they have for years read their newspapers. Uproot them from the house or apartment that has meant "home" for a long time, and you uproot a basic reason for being.

All this is not mere sentimentality, but proven fact. Studies have shown that old folks stay younger and more truly alive in their own homes than elsewhere. In short, many misguided attempts to make declining years easy succeed only in making the decline more rapid.

The tendency to want aging parents to "sell that big old house" or "get out of the apartment" or "stop living alone before something awful happens" is naturally accentuated when only one is left. But it should still be checked. It is never good to rush the season of dependence. Think through whether it is really necessary, now, for your father or mother to give up independence through the loss of its prime basis both in actuality and symbol—his or her own home. Analyze some of the reasons for "can't live alone," which are so frequently given by devoted sons and daughters that they are probably among yours, too.

There is, for example, "Supposing something happened, just think how I'd feel!" What this amounts to, actually, is thinking not in the parents' interest but the child's. In a desire to avoid any future mishap that might make him feel guilty, he wants to make himself psychologically comfortable. If you realize that the price of your comfort is certainly your parents' loss of independence and perhaps of their happiness, you may be inclined to write off this argument.

"They ought to take things easy now and have someone look after them," is a loving but mistaken line of thought. Few indeed are the human beings who at any age want to give up and be tended. Most of us, once infancy is past, definitely enjoy doing for ourselves. Nobody knows whether old horses really enjoy being put out to pasture more than having been in harness, but all the evidence on human beings indicates that old people don't really enjoy being sat or laid down to do nothing but eat and rest. If you feel that an individual and social debt is owed to your parents, remember that it can be better paid through help and encouragement to keep going than through backbone-breaking care which, likely as not, they don't yet require.

Another argument for dislodging aging widows or widowers from their own homes runs something like this: "Mother and Dad were so happy together in that place—she'll grieve and grieve in those surroundings." But never forget, in this connection, that a home full of memories may be even fuller of happy reliving than of sad thoughts of separation.

"Mom never would have any modern improvements, and if she stays in that old-fashioned place she'll work too hard," her children fret. But maybe Mom likes working hard and would be lost without working; and maybe she has her own good reasons for clinging to her old stove rather than, in her seventies, having to master the intricacies of the last word in electric models. Don't make the mistake of putting yourself in other people's places and attributing your own emotions to them. A setup and way of life that seem appalling to you may be just what Mom wants; contrariwise, she might thoroughly dislike the modernity and leisure you think she'd find delightful in your home.

When the surviving parent is male, a common concern is: "But how on earth would Dad ever be able to look after himself, or get his meals? He's never lifted a finger in the house!" For one thing, though Dad may never have done a thing for himself when Mother was on hand to do everything for him, that doesn't mean he's incompetent. For another, there are many little ways in which he can be helped to make out.

This goes for an aging woman living alone as well as for a man, and for couples, too. Any one of dozens of seemingly minor things might make just the difference between an old person's ability and inability to get along in his own home. You will be able to think of many for yourself, adapted to the individual situation of your parents, but here are a few as suggestions. Some may involve financial sacrifice, some sacrifice of time and energy on your part. But bear in mind that in the long run, if they enable your parents to keep on living where they are, they are less expensive than moving, less disruptive of your personal life, and above all invaluable as preventives of premature helplessness.

Even someone to do the heavy cleaning once a week may stave off the need to move. When the Scheldts were provided with a day worker every Friday, their despairing plan to give up their small apartment changed to the joy of "living as we please." They had managed all right until Mrs. Scheldt developed a bad right wrist and she couldn't keep the kitchen and bathroom floors as immaculate as her standards demanded because she could no longer scrub.

But the daily dusting she could still easily do, and she loved puttering about food and the kitchen. If you can possibly afford it, engage someone to do the heavy work. Rightly or wrongly, the old folks will probably have less sense of being dependent and a "burden" if the person who helps them out is hired help and not a daughter, daughter-in-law, or granddaughter.

You might propose sending out the laundry, but if this is against your mother's ideas of how things should be done, don't insist. Likewise, though your father might be benefited by the services of a yard boy, let him carry on personally if he wants to do it. He might be like old Mr. Hewitt, who always had a wonderful time gardening. Every time he did it, it put him to bed for a day—but he said it was worth it.

It would probably be a good idea to have meats and groceries delivered in bad weather, but if your mother has habitually gone to market herself, encourage rather than discourage her from doing so now. Perhaps, having developed her housekeeping habits when freezers were not taken for granted, she will hike up and down the supermarket aisles more frequently than you think sensible (unless you yourself have also reached the age when the Big Weekly Shopping is a mental and physical hazard) but in any case, don't attempt to stop her. She will benefit by being occupied, getting out in the air, and going where she meets people, and you must avoid having your efforts to ease things end up by creating a jail.

When you supply cooked food, be casual and unobvious about it. "We had this for dinner and it was so good I thought maybe you'd like some" does not spell out "I'm afraid you can't take care of yourself." But "I brought this because I was worried that you mightn't have anything to eat" does.

Your parents might utilize one of the "Meals on Wheels" or hot-meals-delivered services under some other name. These range from nutritious meals for the aged poor at little or no charge, to fabulous concoctions, sometimes created at deluxe restaurants, at fabulous prices. The cost of the majority of middle-class-meal-delivery services may be no more than the same meals would cost to produce in one's own kitchen and, indeed, thanks to mass production and no waste because orders based on a choice of menus are given a week in advance, sometimes less. The cost per meal decreases proportionately to the number of days per week the service is used, but at first, even at slightly more expense per meal, your parents might try out the minimum allowable.

The council of social agencies in your community should know where you might find any nonprofit meals-delivered service, and if you look diligently under the heading Catering in your classified telephone book, you may discover a suitable commercial one. Of course you will have to take your parents' food habits and preferences into account when you suggest that they try it. Probably, in this upwardly mobile society, yours are not the same. If the only type of meals they think are really good must include borscht, chopped chicken liver, lox and blintzes, naturally they are not going to go for menus based on *garbanzo* soup, Chicken Valencia, and flan—and vice versa. However, it ought nearly always to be feasible for Mom to prepare something Dad or she craves as a supplement to mass-produced meals, or for you to do so occasionally.

The telephone is another enormous help in allowing the aged to remain in their own homes. See that one is next to the bed. The knowledge that your parents can call you at any time of night without having to get up is reassuring both to them and to you. If you live in the same community, call at a prearranged time once or twice a day just to make sure everything is all right. This is especially helpful to peace of mind if an old person lives all alone.

Should the distance between where you and your parents live make the cost of daily telephoning prohibitive, find out whether there is a volunteer or commercial telephone checking service in their community. At moderate charges, such services make one or more telephone calls a day at specified times. If there is no answer, someone goes at once to find out why and in case of accident or illness sends promptly for medical help. Another telephone checking arrangement is based on the "Buddy" system. Two old people are delegated to call each other, and in doing so their sense of safety and reassurance gets a plus in the gratification of being of service to someone else.

Should a family member or friend not always be available for transportation to church and elsewhere, you might arrange for regular service from a taxicab company, similar to that frequently provided for school children. Specify that you want a trustworthy driver who will, if necessary, help your parents in and out of the cab or up steps.

If it is possible to get homemaker service, it can be a godsend. The great majority of homemakers are women, usually middle-aged, although rather surprisingly a few are men. Homemakers are much more than garden-variety houseworkers or even housekeepers. In addition to doing the chores of cleaning and preparing food they are not only versed in household management, but also in how to adapt to the habits and needs of the particular person or household they are serving. Trained, placed, and supervised by a privately sponsored or public health or welfare agency, they are indoctrinated with the concept that it is more important to help people to help themselves than it is to wait upon them and they can be valuable aides in maintaining an old person's independence as long as possible. Homemakers get guidance from the social worker or nurse to whom they are responsible and report on any emotional or physical problems they may observe. The agency knowledgeably determines whether homemaker service is needed full time, a few hours daily, or a few times a week. Sometimes it is provided long-term and sometimes temporarily, as, for instance, when there is the hard work involved in moving or after someone has returned from a hospital or nursing home.

It was a homemaker who enabled widower Albert Mann and his bachelor twin brother, both in their seventies, to remain in the home they dearly loved, although both were seriously handicapped. Albert was an amputee, confined to his chair; Benjamin was stone deaf. Neither of them knew boiling from broiling, and they had no interest in finding out. The homemaker came three days a week, cooked enough food so that they could manage with leftovers the rest of the time, and perhaps as important, supplied the womanly interest and solicitude both had always received from the late Mrs. Mann. "I wish I'd met her when I was younger!" the bachelor twin chuckled, and Albert, too, was more than happy to be able to stay in the familiar surroundings he had always known.

Although in 1963 there were over three hundred homemaker services and their number continues to grow, the need and demand for homemakers remain vastly greater than the supply. Moreover, some agencies serve exclusively families where there are young children, or recipients of public assistance, or members of a certain religious group. But for all these limitations, before you think it inevitable that your parents uproot themselves, check on what local homemaker service may exist by consulting the national Directory of Homemaker Services published by the U.S. Department of Health, Education and Welfare, Public Health Service, Division of Community Health Services, Washington, D.C. 20201 (price $1.50).

Generally, homemakers do not do the heavy work or laundry expected of a day worker, nor do they render the same kind of services as a practical nurse. There is, however, a category of "home health aides" who, like homemakers, work only under agency auspices. While they are not trained for nursing, what they are qualified to do is render such personal services as help with eating, dressing, grooming, and bathing; preparing and serving special food, and accompanying the old person to the doctor's office or clinic.

Even if your parents require occasional, more skilled care than a home health aide can give, it may still be possible, and indeed desirable, for them to remain in their own home. A visiting professional nurse to give shots, check diet for someone like a diabetic, or give various kinds of treatments may provide just the opportunity for them to live alone. To engage one call the local Visiting Nurse Association or nurses' official registry.

Throughout your thoughtful planning, be careful not to force upon your parents any solution or gadget or service they do not want, or give the impression that you are over-organizing their lives. For many years they have been living in their own way, and even if they stay in their home, superimposed management of their affairs might make them feel dependent. Let your keynote be help without bossiness.

One very important nonmaterial aspect of helping your parents to stay contentedly by themselves is fairly regular visiting by you and other members of your family. The aging need frequent reassurance of affection from their relatives. They are beginning to feel unwanted and unnecessary, and the reminder, in words, that they were once useful and valuable in their homes or to society is no more consoling than a verbal reminder to someone who has lost his money that he used to have it.

Your mother's or father's craving for attention as a token of love may become very wearing. You may be expected to visit daily, and be reproached if you don't. Of course you cannot let your life be controlled by their demands, like that of the unfortunate daughters and daughters-in-law of Mrs. Henry J. Todd, who, from the time she was seventy until she died at ninety, insisted that they bring over sewing and spend every afternoon at her home.

Mrs. Nason's tyranny over her children and in-laws was as formidable, but she operated conversely. She didn't expect them to put themselves out coming to her. She barged in on them continually and assumed that they would not be put out. In vain the younger women in the family begged her to call before she came, to give them a little advance notice, to ask what engagements they had before ringing the doorbell. But Mrs. Nason would become tearful and inquire sadly, "Am I not welcome in my children's homes?" so supinely daughters and daughters-in-law continued to give her her way. But in any case, even if you have to cater somewhat to your parents, remember that what you are doing is far less disruptive than if you all had to live together.

Often, unfortunately, kindly but meddlesome friends or neighbors influence old folks, who, in their heart of hearts, would like nothing so much as to continue having their own homes, into thinking they should sell the furniture and move in with their children. "Now, now, just think how you'll be worrying that daughter of yours if you insist on staying by yourself," one may remark, and another, "Why, anyone would think you didn't get on with your children, the way you don't want to live with any of them!" or "Think of your son living in that big house and poor you all by yourself cooped up in one room."

For many years Mrs. Foster, now eighty-five, had enjoyed herself as much as a solitary and aging woman can, maintaining her own small house near her son's more sizable one. She was in no physical danger, for the family were within call, but there was so much talk in the community about the pathetic old lady who lived by herself and so many people urged her to give up her "foolishness" and "be safe and comfortable" with her son that finally she succumbed. "I did what they told me," she remarked meekly to a new acquaintance after she had made the move; then added, after a long pause, and with no conviction, "Don't you think I was right?"

Instead of acting as an accomplice in this kind of insidious robbery of independence, do everything you can to bolster your parents' confidence in their ability to manage alone. It may not come easy. You will undoubtedly have your worries and, indeed, at times may have to put on an act of cheerful optimism. Do your best to keep anxiety to yourself so your parents don't have to worry about your concern, but at the same time make certain to give them enough assurance of your love and interest to stay on a nice line between fussing and neglect.

Avoid becoming panicky and insisting they must give up their own establishment if they get sick or seem suddenly to be failing. Old folks have their ups and downs to such an extent that in old people's homes it is difficult to classify residents as ambulant or not; those who are bedfast during one season may be walking about the next, and vice versa. In view of the seemingly remarkable comebacks from sickness and infirmity often made by the aging, don't snatch your parents permanently out of the place they love until you have given practical nurses a chance to tide them over. If you cannot afford this service, and they must go where they can get care, at least treat the move only as a trial one.

Annabelle Waring was as difficult and demanding an old lady as ever lived, and the despair of her children because she insisted on staying in her own home. Periodically they would get S. O. S.'s at odd hours of the day or night, have to dash over, and take her away, ill, to one of their homes, for stays that varied from days to weeks to months. Her constant orders, disagreeable disposition and continual interference in every detail of family life invariably frazzled and exhausted them, yet whenever, recovered, she proclaimed her intention of going home, they begged her to stay—happily, for all concerned, without success. To their friends the children deplored the "impossible" situation they had with Mother, entirely overlooking the fact that the periodic upheavals they suffered were definitely preferable to continuous exposure.

Some disabilities that frequently come with age are, of course, permanent handicaps. But sometimes even when these are severe it is possible to avoid an end to independent living. It certainly looked, for example, as though widowed Mrs. Grant wasn't going to be able to continue in the big old house where she and her husband had been happy for forty years. Not only was she so crippled that she could no longer climb stairs, but also the income she had wasn't large enough to enable her to pay for any help. Each of the three Grant sons begged Mother to come and live with him, but Mother had different ideas about what she wanted to do. She rented out the two top floors of her house, which were useless to her, anyway, used the rent money to hire a housekeeper and remained contentedly in her own home until she died. Your mother herself might not have the initiative or determination to solve what seems to be an insoluble problem. But if you think out ways and means and propose them to her, instead of insisting that she give up, there is a good chance that she will welcome your suggestions.

The hazards of some handicaps of old age can be minimized with a little thought. For example, if your mother or father is hard of hearing, make sure that the doorbell has the proper tone and that a telephone extension or jack is placed near the usual place where he or she works or sits. If footing is uncertain, doing away with scatter rugs, polished floors, and anything placed where it can be reached only by a stepladder greatly lessens the danger of falling. Elevators and apparatus for riding instead of walking up stairs are costly to install, but might provide the complete affirmative answer to "Can they get along where they are?"

Always remember, however, that since your parents' home is theirs and not yours, yours isn't the final say about how, where, or what. In short, be an ally in their waning battle for independence without invading their province. If you do your best to see that reasonable allowance is made for infirmities and they refuse to follow your suggestions, you should not upbraid yourself if an accident occurs. A hip broken should be less on your conscience than a spirit broken through enforced dependence.

Perhaps you are thinking, at this point, "Well, that's all very fine for old folks who really want to live alone. My parents talk that way but I'm afraid it's just because they don't want to put us out. Now if I were the right kind of son (or daughter) I'd call the bluff and insist that they move in with us." Spare yourself the torment of such thoughts; just as long as your mother or father say "I don't want to move" or "I don't want to live with my children" you do right to take such statements at their face value and to help them carry out their expressed wish.

One way to defer the painful necessity of their leaving a home they love and going to live with someone else may be for someone else to move in with them.

4

IF ONLY THERE WERE SOMEONE ELSE IN THE HOUSE

ONCE UPON A TIME it would have been relatively simple to find someone to live in your parents' home. There was the Perfect Jewel of a servant who worked a six- or six-and-a-half-day week and never went out at night. Today, not only are few domestic workers willing to live in, but the wages they command for full-time service have risen beyond most householders' means.

Then there was the "lady in reduced circumstances" or "respectable middle-aged woman" who, even without salary was glad to have "a good home." She, too, has largely vanished; nowadays her kind, working in offices or factories, pay for homes of their own. For the same reason the maiden aunt, once available for unpaid service in nearly every family, has likewise become a thing of the past.

Despite these personnel shortages, however, there still remain a variety of possibilities for finding that "somebody else just sleeping there!" who may enable an aging person to remain in his own home, whether he has lived there for fifty years or only a few months.

Perhaps you have an aunt or uncle who would like to move in. When brothers and sisters have always been congenial, often they can have a fine time living together. On the other hand, even though they may have shared happy childhoods, it doesn't always work for elderly close relatives to live together. Everyone is an individual with individual habits and tastes, but older people are individualistic plus; the longer we live, the more we become set in our ways, and our quirks and preferences, far from fading away, become sharpened. If Sister Anne, therefore, has always been an extremely tidy housekeeper and Sister May an extremely untidy one, dearly though they love each other they may get intolerably on each other's nerves. You can only suggest bringing in an aunt or uncle; your parent will have a pretty good idea of how well it might work out, so if he or she is against the idea, drop it.

You might ask your mother or father to consider taking in a stranger. In this case there is more assurance of privacy, for when people are not related it is still easier to retain separating walls, even though they live under the same roof. For thirty years, two retired schoolteachers have been living in the same small apartment in a university neighborhood. They share the kitchen and bathroom but otherwise each goes her own way, and they do not call each other by their first names.

If your parent's home is sizable, or its layout makes feasible some separation of living quarters, a whole family might move in. Such an arrangement lends itself well to juggling the amount of service rendered and the amount of rent paid. Mr. Graham was an elderly man who owned his large, rambling house and, with some income from savings, had no need of additional money. However, because he had a badly crippled hand, he did need a bit of help in dressing and shaving, and wanted to have appetizing meals served to him regularly. The Delano family moved in on a mutually beneficial plan. Mrs. Delano, who had to be at home all day anyway because she had three young children, was delighted to provide some care in exchange for roomy, rent-free quarters for her husband, her children, and herself. Except for a bedroom, sitting room, bath, and a section of the veranda Mr. Graham kept for himself, the Delanos had the run of the house and yard.

Perhaps in addition to needing someone on tap in case of emergency, your parent can stay in his own home only if some money comes in for its maintenance. If little service is needed, some family might be glad to pay rent lower than is current in a comparable type of house because your mother or father occupies one or more of the rooms. Or, at the other extreme, your parent may need a great deal of care for which he or you can well afford to pay. In that case he might pay board to a desirable family which moves into the house where he wants to stay.

The ingenuity of some old people or their children has brought about unusual arrangements that work out very well. Eight years ago, for instance, Anthony Hode was terribly worried about his mother, then aged seventy; but today his worries are a thing of the past. All that she had in the world when her husband died was a tiny income and a large frame house. Mr. Hode, with a large family of his own, was in no position to support two households, so he invited his mother to come and live with him. A positive, healthy woman, she refused, as she also refused equally cordial invitations from her other five children scattered over the United States. She did not, she declared vigorously, want to move out of her home town or, for that matter, out of her house, although she admitted it was too much for her to keep up.

Suddenly, Anthony Hode had a bright idea. He and his brothers and sisters contributed enough money to enable their mother to have the house remodeled into four apartments, one of which provided all the space the elder Mrs. Hode needed for her own living quarters. The others are leased to young couples and, in addition to receiving rent money, Mrs. Hode earns quite a few dollars from baby-sitting. Perhaps more important, she is still happily active—in fact, so much so that this year she would not visit any of her children at Christmas "because one of the tenants might be needing something."

A landlady in quite a different setting is aristocratic little Mrs. Gaylord. She, too, was left at seventy with an inadequate income and, indeed, was worse off than Mrs. Hode, for she had no house. A city dweller, her home for years had been a seven-room apartment for which she could no longer pay the rent. With a heavy heart, she was about to move in with one of her children when a friend suggested, "Why don't you rent out rooms?" Genteel Elinor Gaylord was horrified at the idea of running a rooming house until the friend reminded her that there must be other refined elderly gentlewomen like herself who, since it is difficult for the aging to find living quarters, would be glad to pay a modest rental in a quiet, respectable place.

Today Mrs. Gaylord never lacks for bridge company or congenial conversation when she wants them. Her own bedroom and the kitchen she keeps for herself; all the other rooms are occupied by carefully selected ladies. Whenever there is a vacancy, her children give her the equivalent of the rental until the room is again occupied. The guarantee protects Mrs. Gaylord against worry, and she is happy to take advantage of it, but she is too pleased with her independence to accept any regular allowance.

For men, too, home sharing may work out with amazing success. When eighty-five-year-old Mr. Gary's wife died two years ago, he stubbornly refused to move out of the house in which he had lived for the past forty years. A daughter who lived three blocks away and wanted him to live with her frantically implored him to give up his "crazy idea." But when she saw he was adamant, she suggested that he rent out a room. A thirty-year-old man took up residence, and the daughter heaved a sigh of relief.

But then Mr. Gary went her one better. He proceeded to take in a second roomer—this one a cursing, hard-drinking seventy-nine-year-old character who, since the recent death of his wife, had become the town reprobate. "It will never work!" moaned the children of both. But it did, and still does two years later. The relatively young fellow of eighty-one, feeling proud and responsible, keeps devoted watch over the health of his eighty-seven-year-old landlord. Mr. Gary keeps equally close watch over his junior's morals. "He can't drink in *my* house," he declares, and reform has been effected. Needless to say, the daughter of the former renegade is delighted. She and Mr. Gary's daughter take turns doing the old men's laundry and frequently invite their respective fathers to dinner. Altogether, there are three happy, smooth-running households, instead of two which would certainly have been inconvenienced, perhaps disrupted; also two lively, independent old men who might well have become dreary, disorganized dependents.

No one could have foreseen such a happy outcome of what appeared to be a preposterous setup, so beware a hasty pooh-poohing of your parents' suggestions for housemates. On the other hand, make up your mind that you cannot compel your mother or father to take in someone if the very idea of an outsider in the house is anathema. Some people, old, as well as young, really prefer to live all by themselves.

And some, of course, don't. Indeed, there are some who sincerely believe that the only way they can escape a forlorn and dismal old age is in their children's homes.

5

BUT THEY WON'T LIVE ALONE—OR WILL THEY?

EVEN IF YOUR parents are fearful that they cannot remain by themselves, you should try to dispel this idea rather than encourage dependence. In other words, no matter what they say, unless an extreme health or financial problem exists, living with you ought to be avoided as long as possible.

Women, more often than men, announce their wish, expectation, or intention to move in with their children. And if your mother is one of them, you have a difficult and painful problem. Surely you don't want to say "You can't" or "I won't have you" to your own mother! Surely no matter how thoroughly you are convinced that bringing her into your household is undesirable or unnecessary or both, you don't want to slam the door against a pitiful "Let me live with you, I'm so lonely, and I won't be a bit of trouble," or a cooperative "If we pooled our resources and lived together we'd both have so much more, and I could be such a help to you in the house," or a firm "Well, I've always taken it for granted I'd live with my children if I were left alone, and now I expect to do it."

But you must clear-sightedly penetrate the mist of emotions of love and pity and conscience that tends to engulf you. You must recognize, as your mother cannot, that her very determination to live with you is a danger signal.

Generally speaking, women who want to give up their own households and take refuge in their children's homes fall into two groups. One believes that the time has come to go on the shelf. The other wants to run her children's lives now as she did when they were young. Neither can find happiness in a son's or daughter's home.

Take, for instance, the case of Mrs. Remington. At sixty-four she said she was "resigned to take a back seat." She had lived her life, she declared, and now her only happiness could come from being under the same roof as her beloved children and grandchildren. In her mind's eye she had, like too many of us, a false picture of what constitutes proper behavior for the elderly. According to this concept they should be gentle, retiring, and quiet, content to be mere observers of younger lives and without interests or desires of their own.

"Let me live with you and I'll never interfere," she told her daughter. "I wouldn't think, for instance, of intruding on your family by taking my meals with you—just let me have my dinner on a tray in my room. Don't worry, dear, I won't be any bother. I'll just be my age."

Normally warmhearted, the daughter took her in. But it wasn't very long before both daughter and mother discovered that Mrs. Remington didn't fit into her self-created pattern. She had always been a busy, active woman with a healthy interest in what went on and positive ideas of how things should be done. She wasn't physically bedfast, and just because she had sold her furniture and changed her address she hadn't suddenly become mentally or socially bedfast.

So try as she might to be "sitting with her knitting," like the popular song of the twenties, and to fit into her own ideas of how an old lady living in someone else's home should behave, she could not succeed. Soon she was joining in family activities and giving advice. After all, she couldn't keep quiet when she saw her daughter washing the silver before the glasses, or her son-in-law wearing his trousers too long, or her granddaughter going out with a boy of whom she didn't approve! At first she insisted on eating alone in her room, but it was pretty hard to be upstairs and hear the laughter when there was a dinner party, so after a while she accepted the repeated invitations "not to be foolish and eat with us." Once she was a regular member at the table, why, since she read the newspapers like the rest of them, it was only natural for her to take her own part in heated political discussions and the like.

Little by little, in the household, she became like the camel in the Arab's tent. The camel first said, "My nose is cold; may I put it inside?" Then it was his head, then his forelegs, finally his whole body—and the Arab had to sleep outside. Today, a vigorous seventy-nine-year-old, Caroline Remington remains the same pervasive, omnipresent figure in her daughter's home that she has been almost since the time she was convinced of her readiness to retire from life.

The daughter feels that if only her mother were really happy, she could put up more cheerfully with the situation—her children's resentment at Grandma's ceaseless interference, her husband's tendency to spend evenings at the club because at home he can't read without interruption or take a highball without criticism, her own frazzled nerves because Mother is always at her heels, whether she goes into the kitchen to taste the soup that's cooking or to church to attend a woman's group meeting.

But the sad part of it is that Mrs. Remington, if anything, is the least contented of them all. Living with her daughter hasn't turned out to be anything like what she fondly expected. She hadn't realized, for instance, that the racket and untidiness and perpetual telephoning of teenagers, for a woman her age, were not a spectator pleasure but a confounded nuisance. She never would have thought that her daughter's chain smoking, of which she had always mildly disapproved, could have become so loathsome with constant exposure to the odor of stale tobacco smoke. Above all, she hadn't realized how much she still wanted to be up and doing; here in this home which wasn't hers, she didn't have nearly enough to occupy her, and she was just plain miserably bored.

Marie Muller typifies the other kind of woman who wants to move in with her children because she's "old." Unlike Caroline Remington, she had no delusions about going on the shelf. She wanted to make herself felt, and unconsciously, to keep her power over her son by smothering him back into childhood. When she said, "Well, now it's your turn to take care of me," she was, in effect, attempting to cash in on the investment she had made in him during her younger years.

The son and his wife said to each other, "Of course, since she wants to, we'll have to let Mother move in," and soon they found that they had to let dominating Mother do many other things. To maintain peace, they let her revise the budget and replace their family physician with hers, to have one sheet changed per bed weekly instead of two, and to discharge any maid she did not like even if they did. During periods of being bedfast by minor illnesses like colds she ruled through helplessness, keeping everyone scurrying to serve her.

But no matter how much they let Mother run things, no matter how much they were at her beck and call, they never had the satisfaction and reward of feeling that they made her really happy. This was because it is impossible to go back to the relationship of mother and young child which women like Mrs. Muller crave, and though they may be allowed to take fingers and hands and inches and ells they are bound to feel continually defeated.

Had Mrs. Remington and Mrs. Muller remained in their own homes as long as it was possible, they would, of course, have had some irritations in their relations with their children, and also some frustrations. But they would have been able to work these off by having something to do. What's more, everything between people is magnified and intensified by close living. Even a good relationship between aging parents and adult sons and daughters can be impaired by the day-to-day little things that pile up more friction than the big ones. The cards are stacked against the success of your job when you give in to a parent's insistence on living with you without attempting some other solution—not, of course, necessarily permanent.

The best thing you can do for a mother who wants to give up independent life and attach herself to yours—whether passively, like Marie Muller, or aggressively, like Caroline Remington—is to defer her resignation to "I am old" as long as you can. Open your doors and you are allowing her to renounce independence, as remiss an action as if a nurse allowed a patient to give up eating. Help her to continue for a time under her own roof, and you save her that much dreary waiting for release from a life that has lost much of its meaning.

No book can tell you how to say "No" to your mother if she is asking to live with you. Most of the elderly women who insist on living with their children cannot be made to see merely through reasonable discussion that it is in their own best interests not to do so, and that if they get their way, trouble lies ahead. A skilled family counselor at a family service or similar agency, provided you can induce your mother to see one, is much more likely to enable her to see the situation in proper perspective than you are. Otherwise, your best course is likely to be stalling. Use all your ingenuity to postpone setting a day. You might say, for example, "Well, why not wait until we build on that new room and bath we've talked about?" or "Do you think this is a good time, before your garden blooms?" Make her feel needed and important where she is by such remarks as "Those children next door will certainly miss coming for cookies," or "Whatever will Mrs. Smith do without you? You've been neighbors for thirty years." Assure her, when she dwells on being old, "You're not that old!"

Sometimes parents move themselves into their children's homes insidiously. They may send over some furniture "just to store for me." They may make more and more frequent, more and more prolonged visits. They may play on their sons' or daughters' sympathy. They may get themselves into jams whose most obvious solution is a move into a child's home. There was Mrs. Baum, for instance, who "impulsively" sold all her possessions, terminated the lease of her apartment, and moved into an unattractive hotel room at a rental, she wept to her daughter, she couldn't possibly afford to keep on paying. If you are on guard against such maneuvers and do not succumb to them, you are not being hard-boiled, but sensible and kind, acting in your parent's best interests, quite aside from your own and your family's.

Realistically—and in the last analysis—it is up to you and not to your mother whether she is going to live with you or not. She may say, "I won't live alone." But actually, she is not going to move in with you, and she cannot unless you arrange to have her do so; even the most aggressive old lady is not likely to appear in the vestibule with her luggage and beat at the door until she is admitted. True, you may have to exercise the utmost strength of mind and skill in order to prevent your mother from making the move that is, in effect, a declaration of dependence.

On the other hand, your mother or father or both your parents, even if it has become impracticable for them to remain where they are, may welcome your moral support in remaining essentially independent.

6

A NEW TYPE OF HOME

YOUR PARENTS may say that they want to move, yet still not live with you. Consciously or unconsciously you may feel like opposing their desire to leave the scene where you had a happy childhood and the whole family still gathers on holidays. The sticky sentimentality about the crumbling southern mansion or the old homestead oozed from printed pages and the screen has a valid basis in justifiable sentiment.

But don't forget that obsolete buildings are hard to keep in repair, that one or two aging persons may rattle around in unused space and that a once-pleasant neighborhood may have so deteriorated it is unsafe to go out alone after dark. Whether only one or both your parents are living, there may be good reason to encourage a move to a more compact, easier-to-maintain, better located home. Beware of urging, however, that it be yours!

Perhaps simply to move from a house, even a modern one, to a well-run apartment house will enable them to live more easily and comfortably by themselves. There are no grounds for them to keep up, no trash to take outdoors in all kinds of weather, no responsibility for painting or repairs. A number of apartment houses have markets and other facilities on the premises.

Or, the idea of living mostly in a trailer or mobile home may appeal to your parents. They can tow a trailer with their own car or truck and travel winters to the south, summers to the north. A trailer may be an ideal temporary home for them although you will be most helpful if you call their attention to the drawbacks of life in this modernized covered wagon, for you may be sure that salesmen will stress the advantages. Point out the fact that they will really not be any freer to stop for the night whenever they please than if they stayed at motels, for as a rule they will have to find a trailer park. Where there are great stretches of wilderness, to be sure, they can pull up by the roadside, but still they will be safer to aim for a trailer camp or park.

Mobile homes, which range in size from slightly larger than a train bedroom to the equivalent of apartments with rooms twenty feet wide, cannot be moved by an ordinary car, only by a special service at considerable cost. Often in mobile-home parks there are as many as a dozen families within one hundred feet of each home. Some are populated by renters, not owners. The city-dwelling children of Mr. and Mrs. Foster, from northern Michigan, were horrified when their parents aged seventy-eight and eighty-four, respectively, rented a tiny, inexpensive mobile home in New Mexico. "Why, when Mother stands at the stove her rear end touches the door!" a daughter exclaimed. "And imagine, they have to go out to a community bathroom!" But having been a very hard-working farm wife all her life, Mrs. Foster was delighted to keep house in such limited space, and as for lack of their own indoor plumbing, well, they were used to that and it was certainly less hardship to go out to the bathroom where it was warm and dry than it had been during the long, hard, northern Michigan winters! As for "being on top of the neighbors," which appalled the children, after isolation on a farm the Fosters found that a comforting change. Both became more outgoing and amiable, with each other as well as with others, than they had ever been before.

Whether your parents' background is rural or urban, they may not find mobile-home life as agreeable as the Fosters do. If they are considering it, ask them whether they are sure they will not miss the space for possessions, activities, and occasional getting away from each other to which they have long been accustomed. And having given these warnings and cast these doubts, if they still want a mobile home or a trailer there is nothing more you can do but wish them joy in it.

It is the same story if they are hell-bent on buying or building a new home, probably in a warm, sunny place where they hope to be free of the osteoarthritic twinges that bother most everyone over forty. Your role is merely to caution, not to attempt to control or even persuade. Retired men, especially, equate with paradise the unlimited opportunity to fish, no snow to shovel, and casual dress. Tell your father to beware of the dishonest real-estate operators who play upon old folks' wishful thinking and sell them utterly worthless property sight unseen.

There are also, of course, in the "retirement states" legitimate developers of property who give good value for the money. But their sales talk, albeit honest, is likely to be high-pressure and their picture of climatic advantages over-rosy. They may minimize the need for air conditioning, for instance, and will certainly not mention the monotony of seasons without change.

The humidity which is so relaxing on a vacation, or the dryness which under similar circumstances is vitalizing, can, for some people, become very uncomfortable in prolonged and extreme doses. Propose to your parents that before they pull up stakes they make stays of reasonable length at all seasons in the community where they think of settling. One way to do this less expensively than staying at hotels or motels is to swap homes for a month or two. A few organizations, their names beginning with "Vacation" or "Holiday" specialize in such exchange of homes at quite moderate charges.

Your parents ought also to figure out relative costs of living where they are and where they want to go. Actually some retirement areas are more costly than some industrial cities. The kind of taxes, cost of utilities (even considering less need to heat), and some reserve for traveling to see old friends, children, and grandchildren should be taken into account. While many older people are living happily in the sunshine, others are miserably trapped in it, longing to return to their chilly, smoky old communities but unable to do so because no money is left for another move.

Your parents' move to a warm climate does not necessarily mean, however, that money has to be tied up in their own home. The parents of both Mr. and Mrs. Flaherty wanted to live in Arizona, liked living in houses, but did not have the means to go in for down payments, title closing, and mortgages. Besides, Mrs. Flaherty, Sr., said, "If something, God forbid, happened to either of us there, the other would be stuck with a house."

After a family conference in which all six adults participated, it was decided that the young Flahertys would stake their parents to rentals of a house apiece at a year-round rate little higher than the rate for the "season."

The senior Flahertys have been staying in the same house year after year, but the parents of young Mrs. Flaherty, the Moores, more restless and adventurous, give up their house annually, visit back home during the period no rent has to be paid, and take their chances on being able to rent another house when they return to Arizona.

The children wisely follow a policy of noninterference. If the senior Flahertys don't mind the monotony of staying put, and the Moores prefer to start house hunting all over again each year, that is their business. Anyway, everyone is having fun.

Although they consult you, as you used to consult them, in the last analysis any decision about moving made by your parents must be between them. After all, they worked things out together before you were born and all the years before you were adult. If they move to a new home it will be because both want to; or because your mother is conditioned to the cultural concept that a wife must acquiesce in going wherever her husband decides to go, no matter how much she misses the grandchildren and the "girls" with whom she had regularly played bridge since they were all in high school; or, because, perhaps on medical advice, perhaps on their personal notion that it will help one or both of them to live longer.

By and large, anyone who picks up and starts a whole new kind of life in the later years in a new place tends to be enterprising and self-sufficient. So if you worry about "the folks being so far away from any of us" you may be as surprised as the developer who, via questionnaires, learned from nearly all the prospective elderly purchasers of his houses that they did not want extra bedrooms. "It would only encourage the children to bring their families and pay long visits" was the gist of what they said. Because the trek to retirement communities is so recent, no one can foretell whether these twentieth century migrants will feel as detached and competent to live by themselves as they do now by the time they reach their later seventies, eighties, and nineties. But, as we cannot repeat too often, each step of aging must be considered as it occurs.

During the past few years, retirement "villages" or "communities" have begun to spring up not only in the equable-climate states, but also in almost every part of the country. In addition to those which are commercial, some are religiously sponsored (although not necessarily restricted to members of the sponsoring faith), and some are run by unions or fraternal organizations. They sometimes provide restaurant service and/or medical and nursing care in addition to housing—reassurances to anxious adult children as well as to their parents, who may be beginning not to be up to fending for themselves all the time. The best have a range of facilities to which residents are automatically transferred as the need arises. In one retirement village a mother aged one hundred four is in the nursing home section, a daughter seventy-two occupies a garden apartment, and another daughter, now sixty-one, plans to move into one of the village's detached houses as soon as she retires.

Another way of independent yet somewhat protected living which your parents may elect is a move to one of the apartments especially designed for the elderly. These have many safety features and conveniences, such as nonskid floors and electrical outlets placed where plugs can be attached without having to bend. Often, they have a common dining room and recreation room. Some are part of public housing and restricted to low-income tenants, some are moderate-rental. The apartment house may be philanthropically or municipally sponsored and be nonprofit or it may be commercial; architecturally, it may be garden-type or high-rise. It may be restricted to elderly tenants or it may be a special part of a general housing development. Some old people are happiest living exclusively among one another, and become annoyed if they have to trip over tricycles in the elevators, squeeze by baby carriages in the halls or have their afternoon naps interrupted by the shrill screams of youngsters at play. Others would find life dreary if they could not fraternize with young folks and beam on children. Neither the one kind of setup nor the other is "best." Whichever is better for your parents is simply whatever they prefer.

Big-city apartment hotels have long been a refuge of well-to-do widows tired of the responsibilities of keeping house, of a few elderly bachelors and widowers who have no interest in keeping house, and of older couples who, at no more cost than running a substantial suburban house can continue to live in elegance. Although such hotels have no organized social facilities, older people meet one another (and younger ones, too) in the lobby, elevators, and corridors, and if they do not want to go out in bad weather or bother with cooking in the kitchenette, room service or the restaurant on the premises are available. Before the proportion of older people in our population came to widespread public attention, de luxe apartment hotels were never considered as places where, if they could afford it, they could live independently although with some protection. Yet this is exactly what the long-established luxury apartment hotels are. Always there is a switchboard, and the chambermaid is sure to find out if something goes wrong.

Many of the benefits of apartment-hotel living, like so many things in these United States that were once priced for the few and have been adapted for the many, exist in "retirement hotels." Originally these were nearly always converted old-fashioned hotels where elderly guests could have room, maid service, and meals for very modest rates. Such low-cost retirement hotels still exist and in a few, rates may be lowered still further in exchange for services like answering the telephone or taking care of one's own room. Today there are also brand new retirement hotels with luxury features like indoor swimming pools and cocktail lounges, private baths and kitchenettes with every room, at, of course, correspondingly higher although still middle-class rates, considering all that is included. Some are called "retirement clubs."

Although retirement hotels take no personal responsibility for their guests, who are expected to be able to take care of themselves, they do offer the protection of a group, and employees on the premises. Unlike homes in many retirement communities they involve no capital investment but are on a rental basis. Your parents would be wise not to spend so much of their income on their bed and board that they never feel able to treat themselves to a meal outside, for the same type of food day in and day out even if it is good can become monotonous. Whether or not they live in a housing development for the elderly or retirement hotel in a resort area or in one near old associations, friends, and family, ought not to depend on your anxiety, but on their preference.

Sometimes when a parent is left all alone, or one of the couple is incapacitated or invalided to such an extent that he or she might as well be alone when it comes to help with daily living, distance makes it impossible for children to get to the old people in the major or minor emergencies in which they frequently find themselves. But even if no semi-sheltered living is available nearby, and the handwriting is clear on the wall, "Someday not too far off they'll have to live with us," you do not have to make your parents give up their present independence.

Mrs. Eaton, who lived in Virginia, could not keep dashing out to Oregon where her parents lived every time they needed her. But unlike many daughters, she did not make the mistake of rushing them into living with her. Wisely she helped her mother and father to find an apartment of their own in her neighborhood. Even after her father died the daughter did not sweep her mother into dependence in a household not her own. The old lady moved into an efficiency apartment in the same apartment house in which her daughter lived.

The Albees, who could afford it, set Mr. Albee's mother up in a house of her own just across the road. The Harrises, who could not quite afford two houses, converted the mother's detached garage into an apartment which they rented to several college students. In exchange for reasonable rent (which nevertheless paid the taxes on both houses) they were in turn on call for Mr. Harris' mother whenever she needed help from strong young arms. The Jarretts, who were property-rich but income-poor, could not afford to maintain Mrs. Jarrett's almost penniless mother in the separate establishment both she and they knew was desirable. But as inheritors of a somewhat decrepit though sizable mansion they were able to set her up with a bedroom, living room, and kitchenette in their house. There she cooked, puttered, and entertained as separately as if both families were residents of the same apartment house, and when Mamma went to the "children's" for dinner or the Jarretts to Mamma's, it was as warmly and joyfully as if they lived miles apart.

Another way to help your parents feel free of being a dependent "burden" on you, may be to have them move into someone else's house.

7

IN SOMEONE ELSE'S HOUSE

FOR ONE REASON or another it may really be impossible for your aging parents to maintain full independence in their own home. Yet this need not mean that it is necessary or even desirable to pull them into dependence in yours. Sometimes the happiest possible arrangement for an older man or woman is to have a room or apartment in the home of a relative, friend, or stranger—someone other than a son or daughter.

It's no wonder if this thought strikes you as shocking. For one thing, the idea of boarding care for old folks who have living, responsible children is quite a new one. For another, all our training in filial duty, all the influences of the community, make us assume that we will take in our own. The very idea that Mother or Father could be better off in someone else's home than in ours is little short of horrifying.

It is even carried over into attitudes toward living in the homes of close relatives like brothers or sisters or those of in-laws. When the daughter with whom their mother had been living died, the Tompkins family decided that "she ought not stay on with a son-in-law, even though she wants to and he wants her, when she has living children of her own." But everyone would have been happier had Mom remained where she was. The widower son-in-law missed a housekeeper and an affectionate, interested supervisor of his children. The children missed Granny. The son into whose home she moved and his wife found having an old lady about pretty much of a nuisance, and Mom herself ached longingly for the adored grandchildren who she felt needed her, the son-in-law with whom she was congenial, and the daily contact with memories of the daughter who had died.

To have a parent living with distant relatives or with strangers may be looked on as an even greater sin of filial omission. Nevertheless the fact remains that some aging people who would have great difficulty fitting into their children's homes are having a fine time as boarders. It isn't because they don't love their children or the children don't love them. You can love a person very much indeed, yet still not enjoy living with him for reasons that have nothing to do with sincerity and depth of affection.

Mrs. Thayer, for instance, dearly loved her daughter, an artist who lived in a remodeled barn. But the two had quite different ideas about homemaking. Jeannette Thayer was one of those old-fashioned housekeepers who felt "crawly" if the bathroom floor was not washed every day, the mattresses turned each morning, and the dust carefully removed from the tops of the picture frames, while her idea of "decent" living incorporated crisp, ruffled curtains, shelf stripping, and trousseau bands. The daughter, on the other hand, went in for arty living and sketchy housekeeping. Her furniture was an angular hodgepodge painted mauve and chartreuse; there were cobwebs on the chair legs and rings in the bathtub. For all the love that existed between mother and daughter, Mrs. Thayer simply could not live with equanimity in such surroundings. So after an unsuccessful attempt on the daughter's part to change her ways "to please Mother," Mrs. Thayer sensibly took herself off to board in the "cozy" home of an immaculate Dutch woman.

Another loved and loving parent was seventy-two-year-old Pat Moore, a former railroad brakeman. What's more, he thoroughly approved of his son and was proud of the way he had risen in the world as a businessman. But neither love nor pride in "my boy" made the elder Moore want to move into the younger's suburban home, where dinner was eaten at 7:30 P.M. instead of midday, a butler "watched what you put in your mouth," and "you were afraid to put your feet on the chairs." Contentedly he boarded with a niece in a frame house around the corner from where he had lived most of his life.

Even though their general ways of life may not be dissimilar, it is often harder for aging parents and their children to live together than it would be for either to share a home with someone else. It is quite true that blood is thicker than water, but sometimes its very thickness makes for difficulties. Everything that passes between people as close, yet at the same time, as separate as aging parents and mature children, becomes magnified and intensified by their very relationship. Little tastes and habits which might be tolerable in anyone else can loom large and troubling.

It is one thing, for instance, to laugh over the way old Mrs. Ulrich embarrassed that highfalutin' daughter of hers by cussing out the maid before visitors, but quite another if Mrs. Ulrich is your own mother. You may consider the old gentleman who lives down the street a quaint and harmless, perhaps even charming character, because he dyes his hair and moustache and has an eye for the ladies. But if he were your father, living in your home, you would probably find his appearance and attention to women guests more a cause for distress than amusement.

The tension works both ways. Even if sons and daughters make heroic efforts never to express criticism, their aging parents cannot but feel the need to be on guard in their behavior. It is uncomfortable to suspect that you may be out of place, a misfit, unapproved, when you are only being yourself.

The very fact that most children are chips off the old block is another reason why the chips and the blocks do not always glue well together. None of us can be really detached and objective about either our parents or our children. Both are extensions of ourselves, and in their behavior we are reminded of those of our own traits which we don't want to accept or perhaps even admit. Consequently, almost any human characteristic not necessarily bad in itself can become a source of irritation when parent or child sees it mirrored in the other.

Take, for instance, those habits of spending money which are disparagingly called "extravagant" or "stingy," and admiringly, "generous" or "economical." Daughter may be driven wild by the way Mother squanders, complaining that she is always sending home unneeded gadgets and superfluous stocks of food, while Mother may be equally perturbed by Daughter's equally thoughtless purchases of "bargains" at sales, the careless way she leaves lights burning, and the long-distance calls she makes at 5:50 P.M., when she might as well have waited ten minutes for the night rate. Son may be maddened by Father's "tightness" when the old man comes home exhausted because he wouldn't spend fifty cents for a taxi, while Father may be just as irked by Son's insistence on eating in the kitchen in winter to save the cost of heating the dining room.

Quirks like these, though they might not endear a person to strangers, would be unlikely to become intense issues. But perhaps Mother and Daughter have common memories of a dreadful period when the family was in debt because of its inability to live within its income. Perhaps Father and Son share guilty feelings about Mother, who worked herself into illness for lack of household help and labor-saving machinery which was never bought "because we must save." In any case, much that comes up between aging parents and their children is bound to be a reminder of a thousand previous experiences, and to bring up disturbing emotions of which an outsider is happily free.

This same sharing of common memories often brings about a situation which may in itself seem trivial but which, repeated in daily doses, can add up to a good deal of friction and frustration. Most older people love to reminisce and tell stories, yet when a grown child is present neither can have the satisfaction of being either wholly teller or listener. Accuracy is important to both, and arguments ensue.

When a star boarder in someone else's home launches forth with "I remember when the children were little . . ." nobody knows or cares whether the details are correct. But few sons or daughters can refrain from breaking in on Father when he says, "So Johnny broke his leg right after we moved to the new house," with "But, Dad, we were still in the old house." And it would be practically superhuman to keep quiet in the face of Mother's reiterated praises of her wonderful, devoted son William who always won the prizes at school, when it happened to be you who were the prize winner—not to mention the fact that it's you who have taken Mother in, with William not even willing to contribute to her support.

Distortions of fact which might seem ludicrous if they were not part of your own family history can be infuriating if they are. Wealthy Mrs. Adams, for example, who never had kept house with fewer than three servants in her life, maddened her son with her tales about her heavy labors as a young housewife. He would catch her up on every misstatement, which was a letdown for Mrs. Adams; she was only trying to set a wifely example to encourage her really hard-working, servantless daughter-in-law! The proverbial inability, in short, of a husband to tell a story without supplementation and correction by his wife pales beside the inability of an elderly parent to carry through a narrative in the presence of a grown child. Strangers, though they may not be precisely a captive audience, are at least a comfortably passive one.

Something else that could help your parents to feel more relaxed in a boarding home than with you is the fact that while they probably feel they must continue to teach you, their child, to be duly respectful, obedient, and devoted, they feel no need to try to hold up other relatives or strangers to the right kind of behavior toward them. If a person paid to care for them fails, therefore, to give what they would expect from you, they are in for less of a disappointment.

So will a stranger demand less of your mother or father than you would. Few of us ever really overcome the "Mother knows best" attitude of our childhood, and at forty or fifty we still want her to be as wise as we thought she was when we were seven. Most of us, too, expect more gratitude from our parents than strangers would, and more conformance to our own ideas of what constitutes proper manners and behavior. It is sometimes a downright relief for an aging person to be in a world where his children aren't about telling him what to do, and as a star boarder he may have a fine, free sense of independence.

Many sons and daughters expect their parents to be intensely interested in their affairs. But the fiction "I live only for my children" may be perpetrated and preserved by children as well as by parents. An aging person might not be nearly so eager to live through the lives of his children and grandchildren as the younger ones think, and, left to his own devices, he might be much more concerned with his personal pursuits and activities than with theirs. Aging parents who live in their children's homes not only don't have much choice, except to put up at least a polite show of sharing the family's interests, but also their chances of leading a life of their own are reduced.

Still another advantage of a boarding arrangement is that it is terminable. Each party knows that neither has to go on with it if it isn't satisfactory, so both tend to stay on good behavior.

Of course, if your aging parent wants to board, whether it be in a home, club, or hotel, it must not be just anywhere. It is part of your job to help him or her select the place with great care, to be sure it is suitable and the people in it congenial. The first arrangement may not be the last. The fact that your parent is not happy in one boarding home does not mean that he cannot be happy in another, and there may be some trial and error before you find the home giving just the right combination of protection and freedom, privacy and sociability.

The guidance of a family service agency is important in locating a good boarding home. Its trained case workers are not only qualified to counsel on family situations, but also know places suitable for the aged to live. Some agencies do not stop with recommendations, but follow up with periodic visits by a worker who helps the boarder adjust to the home and the home to the boarder.

Some states require that boarding homes take responsibility for the personal care and recreation of their aged boarders; some require only the same kind of safety and sanitation as is required of hotels. At any rate, however much or little a boarding-home-for-the-aged license may mean, make sure that any you select has one.

More protective than boarding homes, but still likely not to be so protective as the homes of grown children, are foster homes for the aged. Like foster homes for children, these are designed to preserve an intimate family atmosphere rather than one which is institutional. Where they exist, they are chosen and supervised by public welfare departments or Protestant, Catholic, or Jewish social agencies. The foster "children" do for their aging "parents" what the parents' own children would do in the way of personal service, watchfulness over health, provision of transportation and recreation. Although in a foster home an old person is not strictly independent, the agency will see to it that he is helped to feel as independent as possible.

We mention foster-home care largely to indicate the variety of resources for giving a hand to old people outside their own children's homes. The chances of your getting it for your parent, unless circumstances make it absolutely impossible for him to live with you, are rather dim. There are too few foster homes for the aged and too many childless old people.

But in any case, when you encourage your parents to carry out a plan to live in anything from an elegant apartment hotel to a modest boarding home, you need not feel as if you were treating them callously or pushing them out of your life. Whatever the neighbors may say about your parents' "loneliness" or your "selfishness," actually you are helping to maintain, if only for a transitional period until they must become wholly dependent, the fullest life now open to them. You are allowing them to have the opportunity to be among new people and to have a new audience, which is stimulating at any age. You are aiding them to postpone the day when their horizons will be bounded by those of your family. Above all, at the same time as you are assuring them a degree of care and companionship, you are giving them the priceless opportunity to retain some semblance of independence.

All these advantages might also be preserved, although perhaps to a lesser degree, in an old people's home.

8

HOME WITH A CAPITAL *H*

THE IDEA THAT any aging man or woman with living, responsible children should be "sent" or "put" into an old folks' home can bring up repellent visions. Perhaps one pictures a poor little old lady with tears streaming down her withered cheeks being forcibly carted off to a dreary institution. Or perhaps one has in one's mind's eye an equally pitiful old gentleman, who pleads to remain with his son, but is sternly ordered to go where he belongs, among others aged, infirm, and unwanted like himself.

Of course we do not recommend "sending" or "putting" your aging parent anywhere!

What we do maintain is that if going to a home seems to be the practicable thing for your parents to do; if they like the idea; and if, other things being equal, such a move looks as if it would be least disruptive for your family and yourself, it should certainly be considered. It might work out to the advantage of everyone concerned.

Indeed, some old people, if they must give up their own establishments and live with others, would rather be in a home with a capital *H* than a home with a small one. There was, for instance, the old woman whose one hundred and third birthday party, celebrated in a home for the aged, was reported in the newspapers. She had not lived in the home for very long, she told reporters, but had moved in, at her own wish, when she was one hundred, after many years of living with children and grandchildren. "I wanted to live my own life," she said.

Then there was Mr. Hansen, who also moved into a home by his own desire. At seventy-eight, he was well off. He had come to the Midwest many years before as a Scandinavian immigrant, and the business he had founded had prospered. His son, too, had a good income, and for several years after Mrs. Hansen's death, Mr. Hansen occupied a comfortable room in the son's comfortable home.

But, outgoing and gregarious, he was lonely. Most of his cronies had immigrated with him, but they had not gone as far financially, and one by one those who were still living had been trickling into the county home, several miles away. Mr. Hansen began to visit them for an occasional afternoon. Then he took to staying all day. After a while, the visits stretched overnight.

One day, after Mr. Hansen had stayed all of a weekend at the county home, he threw what was a bombshell to his son and daughter-in-law. "It's too much trouble going to see the boys all the time," he announced, "so I've decided I'm going to move in with them."

Wasn't he happy with them, the younger Hansens asked sadly? Why, yes, of course, the old man answered, nobody could have better children; but after all, Sven and Olaf and Eric and he had grown up together. But the county home was for paupers, Mr. and Mrs. Hansen, Jr., protested. He had that all figured out, he said; he wasn't going as a pauper; he intended to pay for his keep and handsomely, too. As for what folks would say—another objection made by his children—well, let 'em say it. And so, despite his son's and daughter-in-law's pleas and protests, off he took himself to the county home as its first paying guest.

Rev. Mr. Thomas Fielding, a retired minister, and his wife, Hannah, likewise preferred life on their own to home life with their children. Their daughter tried frantically to dissuade them "from acting as if you weren't welcome with one of us" but determinedly they arranged to go to a home operated under church auspices. The morning of the day they were to move in the daughter was in tears, but by evening, after she had helped them to get settled, she was a little more cheerful.

"Really," she told her husband, "although of course it's awful to think of Mother and Dad going to a place like that, it's quite pleasant. They have a big, attractive room, and there's a lovely little infirmary, and the dinner was good, and some of the others are retired ministers, too, and they've already been swapping experiences. So, though of course I can't understand their wanting to do such a thing when they know no matter how much it put us out we'd certainly have them live with us, maybe they won't be *too* miserable."

The Fieldings weren't at all miserable. Indeed, after Mr. Fielding died, though the daughter was upset all over again, Mrs. Fielding was determined to stay right where she was. True, the old peoples' home wasn't a full substitute for the home of her own she had had, but it was a very congenial kind of anchorage.

The daughter never fully approved her mother's residence at the home, but gradually she came to see its satisfactions for Hannah Fielding. There she was a personage in her own right. She would pay occasional visits, a few weeks at a time, to her son in one part of the country and her daughter in another, and though she got refreshing changes of scene, she was always happy to return and regale the other old ladies with her doings in the world outside. Even when she was away from the home, it was apparent that her real interests lay with her contemporaries there. Although she would bustle into her daughter's house with "Oh, I'm so eager to be with my dear, dear grandchildren again," she hardly looked at the dear grandchildren after a day or two, and the trend of her conversation showed that she was much more interested in gossip about fellow residents of the home than in the youngsters' bright sayings, noise, and balanced diets. Reluctantly the daughter realized that her mother was enjoying a measure of independent, albeit circumscribed, life of her own, in a world more congenial than the secondhand one of her children.

Now, of course, not all old people prefer to live among others of their own age, for you can no more generalize about "the aged" than you can about "the middle-aged" or "the young" or "children"; all of us at any age are individuals. Some of the aging would be bored to death if they were not habitually exposed to youthful noise and youthful laughter, or if they lacked the stimulation of younger minds and the comings and goings of generations born after theirs. Nevertheless, to others an old people's home offers a haven that best meets their particular needs for some group living, some privacy, a residue of independence, and permanent assurance of care.

Sometimes the assurance of care in such a place can be a

Rock of Gibraltar for either member of an elderly couple who worries about "What ever would happen to him (or her) if something happened to me?" —with no reflection on the children, who, perhaps, have no fixed residence, or are insecure financially, or are more than occupied with the care of a handicapped youngster, or for some other reason seem unlikely to be able to give steady, adequate care to an aged man or woman.

If your parents, for whatever reason of their own, are among those who really want to go to a home, the best thing you can do for them is to help them be happy in doing so. If you raise objections to their plans, bombard them with arguments as to why this would be an unthinkable move, or act grieved that they do not want to live with you, you put a burden upon them. It takes even more firmness and courage for a parent, especially one who is growing old, to insist on doing what he wants in the face of a child's disapproval or disappointment than the other way around; so if your mother or father think that their preferences make you angry or ashamed or weighed down by guilt, they cannot enjoy carrying them out. The need for being loved does not diminish with age; if anything, it increases, and the fear of losing his children's love can become, for an aging person, an all-pervading, almost constant terror. Rather than displease or hurt you, your parents may give up cherished plans, and so, in effect, give up life itself; it is as if a veteran sea captain handed over the wheel to a junior in tacit acknowledgment that he was no longer capable of steering his ship's course.

But cheerful assent is by no means all you can do to further your parents' life in a home as a happy experience. It is an important part of your job to help them to select the one which is right for them. The majority of private homes for old folks, and some public ones, are good. But others are undesirable, unpleasant, and depressing. It is up to you to investigate and make certain that the home to which your parent is going is one that will provide not only good care and attractive surroundings, but also will help to keep him or her alive in more than body.

A social worker connected with a family service or welfare agency can be very helpful in evaluating homes for older people. But even if the services of a social worker are not available, there are certain criteria you yourself can apply.

Is the home physically pleasant, clean, comfortably—not necessarily luxuriously—furnished, well-ventilated, and well enough lighted for failing eyes? Is the food good? Ask to see a week's menus, or, better still, sample a meal. What provisions are there for medical care, and is it always available promptly? Is there a cheerful, well-equipped infirmary in case of minor illness? A nursing section for prolonged illness? In case of acute illness, is there automatic provision for hospitalization and return to the home afterwards?

Do residents of the home have backgrounds similar to your parents? Living day in and day out with the same people, your mother or father could be very miserable among others who were uncomfortably far above or below them in manners and social station.

Is the home conveniently located to churches, shopping, and theaters? Do residents have freedom to come and go as they please, or are they hemmed in with a mass of rules, regulations, and restrictions? A certain amount of adaptation is, of course, inevitable whenever people live in a group, but remember that an undue amount will be even harder upon your parents than it would be on you. They have had more years behind them of not accounting for every little move or saying "by your leave." In an excellent Jewish home for the aged, where each resident has a small refrigerator in the bedroom, individuality is so greatly respected that despite the fact that the home's kitchen is run according to Jewish dietary laws, no one objects when ham for snacks is kept in the refrigerator. Similarly a fine Catholic home allows for individual preferences by having a bar. "These people had cocktails in their own home every evening," says the Mother Superior heading it, "so just because they are on in years, why should they be deprived of something to which they are accustomed and enjoy?" The dining room tables of an equally good Methodist home are steadily cluttered with glass jars. Residents may keep their own particular favorite preserves and relishes always at the tables where they eat.

May couples room together? Will either or both your parents have their own room, where they may have at least some of their own belongings? In the better old people's homes, one needs only to glance into a bedroom to learn whether the occupant is a man or a woman, a plant lover or a book lover, a member of the clutter-makes-coziness school or someone who severely eschews anything not actually needed. Quarters in inferior ones, however adequately furnished, have as little individuality as barracks.

What does the home provide in the way of entertainment and occupation? Are there parties? May residents have guests? Are women encouraged to do needlecraft and other handiwork? Is there a workshop for men? Is there any kind of self-government organization for the residents? Are there a glee club, a band, and the like? Is there provision for going to church, synagogue, or temple, or is worship restricted to services conducted within the institution? May residents earn money for something they make, or for services in the community such as tutoring or baby-sitting? In short, is there a consistent, deliberate program for stimulating residents to remain interested and alive? Without one, aging residents of homes all too easily sink back into a mere waiting to die.

Of course, even if you have visited and found a home which meets with your parents' and your approval, it may not be possible for them to go there. Unhappily, almost all the good homes for older people not only have very definite and sometimes very narrowly restricted admission requirements, but also long waiting lists. Also, you may not be able to meet the continuing charges of a private home of this type—nowadays, with the rising cost of living, fewer homes accept residents by way of endowments than formerly—or, on the other hand, you or your parents may be too well off for eligibility for a public home. Nevertheless, you cannot tell what the chances of admission are until you try.

In any case, the earlier application is made for your parents' admission to the home of their first preference, the better. Often the very reassurance that there is a place to go in case of future need prevents the need from occurring. And of course it goes without saying that if your parents decide to go to a home, you should read carefully anything they are asked to sign, in consultation with a lawyer.

Once your parents are living in such a home, visit and be visited as if they were still in their own home with a small *h*. The more you can help them to feel really at home in this new situation, the more at home they will be, and the more independent they will feel in a world that is still theirs, not a shadow of yours.

Even if they are already living with you, it may not be too late for them to go forth on their own.

9

BUT IT'S TOO LATE NOW—OR IS IT?

CERTAINLY IT IS much harder to change a situation which already exists than it is to prevent it. But too many sons and daughters continue or compound a mistake with the defeatist attitude, "It's too late now to do anything about it." This is especially true when well-meaning children impulsively take lonely, bewildered, or ailing parents into their homes and then, although in time everyone concerned may be miserable, no one opens the doors to escape.

When the Levys took Alma Levy's recently widowed mother, Helen Asher, into their small apartment with them, she was sixty-six, grief-stricken, and having a flare-up of her chronic arthritis. Because she was unhappy and aching, they lovingly assured her that she had no need to continue with her job as secretary to Henry Housman, a topflight lawyer who was eager to keep her on with him as long as possible regardless of retirement-age conventions. Crushed, weary and grateful, Mrs. Asher exchanged her substantial salary for a modest social security income, sold her furniture for a pittance, and moved into a day bed in the Levys' living room. Now, five years later, three individuals feel trapped and frustrated. Mrs. Asher misses her stimulating work and contacts and her own home. The Levys miss their former privacy and freedom. They don't like the impossibility of having company if Mama wants to go to bed, or the fact that they feel so sorry for her they are reluctant even to go out for the evening. The situation is similar to the ones in plays wherein everyone is miserable over a misunderstanding which could be cleared up by a few words from some of the characters. Just as no one speaks these until near the end of the third act so the Levys and Helen Asher kept silent about their wish to live apart.

Yet for several years it would probably have been feasible for Helen Asher to have gone on her own again. Her arthritis, which has become worse with idleness and despondency, need never have become as physically or emotionally crippling had her daughter and son-in-law seen to it that she got out of the apartment and went regularly to the excellent rehabilitation clinic in the community. Her income could have been sufficient for her to live alone as she did before, for her former boss now eighty, still practicing, and complaining about the incompetent young things he has to hire and fire nowadays, would doubtless be delighted to take her back if she suggested it.

A few words from Mrs. Asher's daughter to the effect that "It must be pretty lonely for you here, with both of us working" and "Maybe getting out to the clinic would help your arthritis" and "I wonder how Mr. Housman is managing without you" might break the logjam of Mrs. Asher's fear of hurting her dear, kind children by suggesting that she was not entirely happy in their home. But the words are not said because the Levys are equally afraid to hurt Mama.

Similarly Mrs. Herrick and her daughter Sandra love, harass, and mistakenly spare each other. In their case Mrs. Herrick's precipitate move into her divorced daughter's home was because of a financial crisis at the tail end of the Great Depression. At the time Sandra was in her early thirties, living on meager alimony and a low-paying job in a department store; Mrs. Herrick, in her fifties, had been speculating and had little left but some then worthless pieces of paper. It was sensible if not essential for them to double up at the time, so Mrs. Herrick moved into Sandra's apartment.

They never quarreled openly, but neither really enjoyed living with the other. Mrs. Herrick disapproved silently but manifestly of Sandra's men friends, the hours she kept, the kind of food she served, the amount she drank, and the length of time she spent at the telephone. Sandra felt certain that the reason she didn't have the chance to remarry was because of her mother's continual, inhibiting presence.

In time the securities Mrs. Herrick still held began to be valuable again, and with prudent reinvestment she became well off financially. Meanwhile Sandra had been repeatedly promoted until she became an executive with a very large salary. The time when they should have amicably separated and each moved into her own apartment to live in her own way was when each could live comfortably alone. But each lacked the courage to broach the subject with the other, so with Mrs. Herrick now in the eighties and Sandra in her sixties they are still sharing a home and still getting on each other's nerves.

Maria Santini did have the courage to arrange for her father's living outside her home after he had been in it for several years, but attained it only when her husband threatened to move out if the old man did not. With no life of his own in his daughter's household, old Mr. Carino had nothing to do but throw his weight around and make bids for attention. Hot-tempered and tyrannical with the children, so demanding with his daughter that it was impossible for her to have any life of her own, critical of his son-in-law, he dominated what was anything but a happy home. When, with the help and encouragement of a caseworker, a boarding home was found for him, he raged over being "thrown out." But, although Maria was anguished, she went through with the plan.

Tormented by guilt, she determined to spend every afternoon with her father. The first time she visited, he berated her; the second, he sulked; the third he was a little more pleasant and the fourth he was really pleasant but asked her, about an hour before the time she usually left, whether she didn't want to go home to be with the children. Astonished by more consideration than he had ever shown when he lived with her, Maria was still more astonished during the next visit. Something seemed to be on his mind, and ultimately he came out with it. "Maria," he said, "you know, I wish you wouldn't visit so often and stay so long. The fellows here play cards every afternoon and I'd like to be free to join them." It wasn't long before Mr. Carino began to be the affectionate father Maria remembered from her childhood.

Some families make it difficult for their aging parents to leave after they have come for what is supposed to be only a long visit, or during convalescence, or after bereavement. For their sakes the children may move to an apartment with another bedroom or to a house all on one floor and then, wouldn't I be acting ungracious and ungrateful, Mom and Dad feel, if I said I wanted to go?

Instead of simply assuming that your parent wants to keep on living with you, you would do well to sensitize yourself to any and all indications that he might welcome some other living arrangement. At any rate, if you are feeling uncomfortable in the current one, you can be fairly sure that he is too.

Occasionally two or more adult generations feel stuck together not because the older one has moved in with the younger, but the converse. The Spellmans married when they were young and poor and lived with her parents who were able to give them a much more comfortable home than Jim Spellman could provide. Nothing prevented their establishing their own home when Jim began doing well in business but the older couple were reluctant to say "Move out" and the younger one "Now that we can afford it we'll leave you." Respectively in their fifties and seventies, they are still living together and wishing they were living apart.

When the Harold Talbots doubled up in his parents' home it was not for the benefit of the younger couple but, they thought, for his mother's. Harold was an only child, and his father was in a hospital, dying of cancer. "It will only be for a little while," he told his bride, "and Mother is so upset—would you mind if we waited to get our own place as long as Father is alive?" She felt that she must say yes so in they moved with her mother-in-law. But it was not only for "a little while." It has turned out to be for keeps. Harold felt that after his father had died they ought to stay a while longer to tide Mother over her initial grief. Then "Mother will be so lonely if we leave her," then "Mother isn't getting any younger," and now it is "Mother's old and is so used to having us with her this is certainly no time to walk out on her."

Meanwhile there would have been time after time when Mother Talbot, although she might have wept about "losing" her son, thereby making him feel guilty, would have been better off without the younger Talbots in her home; for instance when she would have liked to exchange her large house for a small apartment but couldn't because she was not alone; when the babies came, four of them in six years, and so many small children crying, quarreling, and getting into things overwhelmed her; or when her sister, with whom she was much more congenial than she was with her daughter-in-law, also became a widow and the two of them under other circumstances could have very pleasantly lived together.

All this is not to suggest that it is never desirable for parents and grown children to live together. When one of the generations moves into the other's home, everything depends on what the parent is like, what the child and child's family are like, finances, and the particular situation.

PART III

You Live Together

10

PREVIEW OF DOUBLING UP

Now we assume that you have reviewed every possibility for your parents' living apart from you, yet still you find that you must live together. Or perhaps for months or years one or more plans have been tried to keep them living independently, but the time has come when none is feasible. It is inevitable that one of you will have to move in with the other.

The old folks are very likely to say—and to believe what they're saying—"Now there's nothing at all to worry about. We always did get along all right, didn't we? And so we shall still." But you, as the more clear-sighted of the two generations, will need to recognize that for two individuals or two sets of people in maturity and late maturity, respectively, to make readjustments in their way of living is not as simple as all that. Drastic rearrangements of almost every phase of your present day-by-day life are inevitably involved. The more frankly, therefore, you face certain facts about doubling up beforehand, the fewer unpleasant surprises you will have and the more smoothly things will run along.

These facts are neither good nor bad in themselves: they are just facts.

One of them is that the old saying "No house is big enough for two women" is quite true. Mother or daughter or daughter-in-law is—and must be acknowledged mistress of the household. In the days before China became a Communist nation, if you had belonged to an orthodox Chinese family there would have been no question about the head of the household. The Chinese expected and accepted the fact that the older woman in the family should rule. But you do not live in ancient or modern China, and in the United States where there is no such fixed code, each combination of generations living under one roof has to work out its own regime. Realize that no matter how much amiable conversation you have with your parents about "sharing expenses" or "working out the housekeeping together" or "taking turns at running the house" one of you is definitely going to be living with the other, and you will avoid much of the friction bound to result from deluding yourself that management of the home you both occupy could be fifty-fifty.

Whether you move in with your parents or they with you will probably be determined by the respective amount of physical space available in the two places you have been living. But in any case, who moves in with whom will influence the relationship of the generations.

Many aging parents cling to a "big old house" as a talking point for gathering the family round once more, or have always expected their children "to come back home again someday." This is all right if you realize what is happening and why and its effects. Your parents cannot really reconstitute the family with any more success than food processors have actually reconstituted eggs. The family can no more be what it was when you and your parents were younger than a powdered egg is a real egg. Instead it will be something new, made up of the same ingredients as formerly, to be sure, yet anything but a perfect reproduction.

If you move into your parents' house, they will have a tendency to treat you as a child again and you to act like one in relation to them. Be prepared, therefore, both for your mother's or father's attempts to direct you as they did when you were small, and your own inclination to ask them what to do. You might, to your own astonishment, find yourself asking your father whether you ought to prune now or later, or your mother whether she thinks that material could be cleaned or ought to be washed, although for many years now you have been making such far-from-momentous decisions all by yourself.

Recognize your parents' reversion to parental attitudes of your childhood for what they are and you may be able to find them more amusing than infuriating. "I declare, Mary, you wouldn't ever eat a full meal if I weren't here to see that you did," your mother may tell you. Or you might overhear your father saying to a neighbor, "That boy of mine's a fine boy, but if I didn't keep an eye on his investments he'd run the whole family into the poorhouse."

Although an unrealistic return to earlier relationships could occur if your parents move in with you, it is more likely to do so if you move in with them. Living again in their house acts as a kind of trigger to set off old associations, many of them quite pleasant for both parties. To your parents, your childhood, when you were living with them before, was a period when there was life in the house and something was always happening. To you it was a time when you were sheltered. It is understandable why you both might unconsciously want to return to those happy times. But consciously, you need to realize that you cannot. You will all get along better if you do not maintain the fiction that the present is the past.

Something else likely to happen if you move in with your parents is their assumption of the role of master and mistress, host and hostess. No matter how much they talk about turning over the management of finances, the household, and whatnot to you, and no matter how sincerely they believe their own talk, the chances are very remote that they will do so. Indeed, someday you need not be surprised if they indicate that you moved in on them as an invader, or, instead of being grateful to you for coming to them, patronizingly inform you that "we gave you a home." This kind of thing is not easy to take at best, but at least the knowledge that it can be expected is a kind of shock absorber.

Remember that no matter how much your parents need to have you with them, or, for that matter, how much they think they want you at the time you move in, the new setup is not going to be wholly easy for them. You will disturb the even tenor of their ways. When for years they have lived in elderly quiet, they will almost certainly be bothered by an inevitable amount of noise and confusion if you have children, and some even if you do not. You may keep the shades up or down when they have been used to having them down or up, or the salt at the left or the right when they have always stood it at the right or the left, or the lawnmower an inch higher or lower than where they have been setting it. These are little things, but repeated and added together they can become catastrophic.

Perhaps your timing is entirely different from your parents'. You might have a "mañana" attitude, they one of "do it now"; or, equally upsetting to their long-established way of doing things, it may be the other way around. Perhaps your habits are quite unlike theirs. On Sundays they go in for 1:30 dinners complete with chicken and ice cream, while you like brunch; they go to church, you play golf. Your mother prefers to have the bedrooms in order first; your way is to begin with the living room. Your father regularly wants to watch TV comedians at just the times you want commentators. Again these differences in tastes or ways of life are apparently trivial. But when they unbalance a household that has been sailing along in the same way for decades, they can take on the nature of a shipwreck.

Withal, there are certain values for your parents in having the doubling up in their home. They remain in dear, familiar surroundings. They are spared the wrench of saying goodbye to the bulk of their possessions, not to mention the agonies of that emotional equivalent of grave digging, going through and throwing out the accumulation in the attic. Material things which are their own and to which they are accustomed can be very important to your parents' comfort and happiness. But there is also a less tangible advantage for them in having you move in with them rather than they with you. They can still retain some of that sense of being needed which is vitalizing for any of us.

To most sons and daughters there are obvious advantages in having their parents move in with them rather than having to move in with their parents. Nevertheless, sometimes the inevitable inconveniences that result from "taking in Mother" (or Father) obscure the fact that uprooting themselves and their families to bring about living together would be even worse.

If your parents are going to move in with you, you can expect similar situations in the way of emotional reactions and discomfiting differences in habits. But the emphasis is likely to be not quite the same.

For instance, though the old parent-child relationships will probably be stirred up, the chances are they will be less strong than if you were to move in with your parents. Mother may feel impelled to tell you want to do—"Tomato sauce, my dear, shouldn't be mixed *into* the meat loaf; it should be served separately"—but her instructions will be more those of an adviser than of the mistress of the kitchen. Dad may express positive ideas as to when the lawn should be seeded, but he will act more like a straw boss than a real one; he would be far more positive if he were convinced *his* lawn was about to go to wrack and ruin.

As for your own reactions, probably they will be more akin to those of your adolescence than to those of your childhood. Because in your own home you have constant reminders of your maturity and independent adult life, your return to a seven- to twelve-year-old attitude toward your parents will tend to be checked. If you do slip partially back into some earlier relationship it is more likely to be that of your teens. Then you were still dependent on your parents, to be sure, but nevertheless had a drive to act on your own and really were responsible, hard though it was for your father and mother to believe.

Whether you live with your parents or they with you your relations with your husband or wife will inevitably be put under a strain. This, we realize, is a pretty flat statement, and your first reaction to it may be an indignant "Well, that wouldn't be true with us—nobody could be sweeter and less interfering than they" or "It couldn't possibly make any difference having Dad in the house; he'll be as interested in going about his business as we are in ours."

But stop to think a little and you cannot but recognize that by having a parent in the house you are bound to sacrifice some conjugal privacy. Often you will have to wait until your bedroom door is closed at night to discuss subjects like the precarious state of your finances or the children's unsatisfactory report cards or whether that promotion is really going to come through—matters which, in their own way, are almost as intimate, as exclusively a husband's and wife's, as sex relations. You will always have the fear that your quarrels, minor or major, may be overheard. You will have decreased opportunities to freely let off the steam which accumulates in even the happiest marriages.

If an argument does take place before your parents they would be superhuman if they never took sides. At best, they will probably proffer amiable and unwelcome advice; at worst, sharp criticism of whoever is the in-law, and who never was good enough for "my" son or daughter anyway. If the son- or daughter-in-law should immediately or later criticize the parent, daughter or son is likely to become defensive about "my mother" (or "my father"), who really is "just as good as yours." Where emotional ties between husband and wife are already none too strong, such tensions can bring about an open break.

We would be delighted to be able to tell you that awareness of the likelihood of your parents' causing difficulties between you and your husband or wife can entirely prevent them. But unfortunately there are almost certain to be what in international parlance are called "incidents." Knowing what you will be up against, however, can help greatly in preserving the peace with the man or woman to whom you are married. You will recognize the ructions created by your parents' presence as mere skirmishes and not mistake them for major battles in a marriage that is basically sound.

A common problem when families double up, whether in the home of the older or the younger generation, has to do with living space. Usually it is most evident and acute when parents move into their children's homes.

One of the most important things for you to think through thoroughly before you take your parents in to live with you, therefore, is this very practical but too often unconsidered matter. No matter how you look at it, no matter how roomy your house may be, no matter how willing you are to have your mother or father or both become part of your household, the fact remains that the addition of one or two individuals will mean that much less room for the rest of you. When people at a party are sitting, talking, in a circle of chairs, and more guests arrive, some of the chairs are going to have to be shifted to make a place for them. It is as simple as that, yet sons and daughters in the flush of enthusiasm or panic over taking in their aging parents have a way of forgetting an elementary law of physics—that two objects cannot occupy the same place at the same time.

Face the facts in advance, anticipate readjustments, and you will be better able to take them in your stride than if they come as a succession of disagreeable little shocks. Realize that the new space limitations which your parents' presence is bound to impose on you and your family will not just be temporary. It isn't the same thing at all to have Grandpa occupying the guest room for a two weeks' visit and to have him permanently installed, to the total exclusion of house guests.

Bear in mind, too, that the space a person requires takes in more than a bedroom. Your parents will take up space in the living room, for instance; in an easy chair or beside a reading lamp or stretched out on a couch during naps. There will be another chair occupied and another place set at the dining room table. The hall closet will contain more coats and more overshoes and another umbrella. The contents of the refrigerator will not only be increased certainly by provisions for one or two more persons, but very likely also by special little foods. Grandma, for example, may like buttermilk, or Grandpa enjoy having some favorite smelly cheese always in the house.

Nothing we write and nothing you do can increase inches or feet of space in your home. But if you accept beforehand the fact that your family as it will be is not going to have the same amount of space at its disposal as the family that was, the irritation of finding Dad in your favorite armchair when you come home or having to rearrange the kitchen closet to make room for Mom's assortment of teas will be lessened. No one who starts off on a trip with a reasonably full, nicely packed suitcase is angrily surprised when he finds that it can't be packed as easily or well if he adds purchases en route. Yet families are naively astonished when they learn from experience that another person added to a household makes it impossible to live exactly as before, and often the discovery creates the first frictions between the generations.

Space and time both are involved in the familiar familial Battle of the Bathroom. Maybe the early-morning rush hour has been bad enough, with Daddy having to get off to work and the children off to school. One or two more participants are bound to make it that much worse.

The temperature at which you keep your home can become a real issue. And then there is the matter of food likes and dislikes. Few things are more disgruntling to a daughter or daughter-in-law trying her level best, with painstakingly prepared dishes, to please the aging person who lives with her, than to be greeted with a sullen or plaintive "I don't eat liver," "I'm allergic to salmon," or "I never like anything cooked with onions."

Don't fool yourself that all these are just unimportant "little things" which will melt and blend like bits of chocolate in a warm sweet sauce of mutual affection. They are the very stuff of daily living and with repetition can become big and important. Indeed, almost more than anything else, they can make or break the happiness of everyone in a home and the ease and efficacy of your job of caring for your parents.

Give as much thought to how you are going to work them out as to other things which you may have heard are essential in helping the aged to lead full, contented lives, such as making arrangements to get them to church or seeing that they have hobbies. In advance, talk over with your parents who is going to make what concessions. When you live together, some will certainly have to be made by someone—and not necessarily always by the younger people.

For example, in the matter of occupying the bathroom, have a clear understanding with Grandma or Grandpa that they are *not* going to be able to take their baths on arising, even though that is the time they have always preferred, because in the early morning the bathroom must be kept free as possible for the working and school-going members of the household. On the other hand, the old folks must not be the only ones regulated. The children must understand, for instance, that whatever period is reserved for your parents' bathing is not the time for bathtub boat sailing.

Then, too, before you actually double up, find out what your parents like and don't like to eat. You need not drastically revise your family's eating habits in order to cater to them, but you will find it much less disrupting to be able to plan ahead to give them eggs when you have a meat dish your family loves but they won't eat, than it is to have to whip up a substitute when a pained look or cross refusal occurs at serving time. Likewise, if you give your parents advance information about the kind of food your family likes, which dishes will appear often on the table and which seldom, they will be spared surprise disappointments.

When it comes to such other details as the brightness or dimness, the coolness or warmth at which rooms are kept, make up your mind that both you and your parents are too old really to alter your preferences. So, since neither of you can go on having everything exactly the way you want it, one will sometimes have to give in to the other. Decide what things, no matter how trivial they may seem, are sufficiently important to require a definite understanding that this is the way it is going to be.

Then proceed to have that understanding. It can be clearly,

amiably, and thoughtfully reached in one or more pre-living-together conferences cooperatively held by you, your family, and your parents. It is an excellent idea to take down in black and white the conclusions, decisions, and agreements reached at these discussions. Sentimentality may make you recoil from the idea of "anything in writing" between people so close and dear to one another as parents and children, but good sense should make you see the advantages. Later, should any issue arise, a quiet "Now, let's see, didn't we decide we'd do this thus and so?" will be better than any amount of nagging and quarreling.

Families who foresee the need for making the many real adjustments that unavoidably must be made with doubling up, and who have advance agreements clearly understood and accepted by all parties concerned, start off living together with the odds in their favor. They enter upon their new way of life as calm adult individuals who, with their eyes open, undertake a long-term project, rather than as emotional Samaritans excitedly taking in excited victims of a flood. Obviously something that involves the rearrangement of two or three or more lives for an indefinite period merits and, indeed, requires thoughtful planning and careful analysis.

As the rewards of such forethought, no one can promise that the road along which you and your parents henceforth travel will always be smooth. But this much is certain: by knowing the rough spots and as much as possible being prepared for them before you set forth, you can avoid not only many bumps and jars but also, perhaps, even a smashup.

Should you have brothers and sisters, another important forethought is to be sure that they are in on all plans concerning your parents.

11

THE SHARE OF YOUR BROTHERS AND SISTERS

IF YOU ARE AN only child just skip this chapter. But if you have siblings—brothers or sisters—it is for you. They have an important part in planning for your parents, even though you may be the one with whom your mother or father lives.

A great many words could be written on the duty and morality of sons' and daughters' fair sharing of responsibility for their aging parents. It would be easy to expatiate on what each one *ought* to contribute. What's more, you could probably add plenty of words of your own about what you *want* your siblings to do for and about your parents. But here again, as in making decisions about living arrangements, the only realistic consideration is what *can* be done.

In the Naylor family, for instance, son-in-law Tom is unemployable because he has multiple sclerosis and his wife is struggling to support and care for him and six children. It goes without saying that she can give nothing either in the way of financial help or personal service to her mother or the sister with whom her mother lives. Then there is the Riggs family, in which the eldest sibling, Bill, hasn't talked either to his father or brothers or sisters in over twenty years. Nobody could expect Bill to re-enter the family picture with a sweet smile just because old Mr. Riggs now needs care and support.

Subtler factors, too, sometimes throw a realistic monkey wrench into what might be ideal justice. Because of personality differences some people go ahead and do what is generally considered "the right thing by their parents," while others lie down on the job. In an occasional family—and yours may be one of these—one or more individuals consciously avoid taking any financial or emotional responsibilities toward Father or Mother, or, for that matter, anyone who might be a dependent. *King Lear,* as everyone knows, is a classic story of children's unkindness to a parent.

The reasons for unloving children's callous behavior go way back to family relationships in their childhoods. So do the reasons for the loving ones' devotion. Cordelia, youngest of King Lear's daughters and the only one who was good to him in his old age, had been his favorite as a child: "I loved her most," he says early in the play. So although one feels sorry for him when his two older daughters, Goneril and Regan, ill-treat him, at the same time one must recognize that their very behavior is evidence of his failure to have established as good a relationship with them as with Cordelia. The Gonerils and Regans in your family, if there are any, were cast for their roles long before any of you needed to play parts in the last scenes of your parents' lives. You can therefore save yourself much futile exasperation if you don't delude yourself that at this late date you or anyone else can get them to change the way they act.

Fortunately, however, most people are not villainous, but filial-minded and basically decent. So if you give your siblings half a chance probably they will share in your job as they are able. When one child in a family shoulders the entire load of an aging parent's care, usually it is because consciously or unconsciously he ignores or shakes off potentially helping hands.

Take, for example, the case of Marian Benton, who had three siblings but assumed exclusive responsibility for her father. When he had to sell his home, she whisked him into hers without consulting any of the others. Nor, at any time later, did she attempt to take her brother and sisters into plans for their parent. It was she who handled the investment of the small sum he got for the house and she who arranged for his regular medical check-ups.

When a well-to-do brother offered to send Dad an allowance, Mrs. Benton stated proudly and stiffly that really it wasn't necessary, Dad had everything he needed. When an older sister suggested that Dad stay with her for the summer "as a change for him and a rest for you" Marian said thank you, but it might upset him to be uprooted. When a younger one wanted to hold that year's Thanksgiving family reunion at her home, Mrs. Benton countered with an invitation to "come here, so Dad won't have to travel." Gradually, like a husband who stops offering to help his wife with the housework because of frequent rebuffs based on his incompetence, Marian Benton's siblings grew discouraged. In time, about all that they did for their father was call on him.

Mrs. Benton's friends were all very sorry for her and quite indignant at her siblings. It wasn't right, they told her, with two sisters and a brother, that she should be the only one tied down and straitened. Marian made no secret of the fact that she carried a heavy burden. "But what can I do?" she would remark with a martyred little sigh. "Somebody has to look after him and the others just don't."

Whenever one child similarly carries the whole load of an aging parent's care, it is usual enough to hear "how unfair it is." It is much less usual to hear about how unfair it is for one child to appropriate that load and thereby distort a collective responsibility into a monopoly. The situation is unfair to siblings, whom it makes feel guilty and a little resentful. It is unfair to parents because it robs them of a close relationship with their other children.

If you believe that you alone have the responsibility for your parents, ask yourself this question: "Is it really because of inexorable outer circumstances, or because of something in me?"

Do you, for instance, so much need to be needed that you are afraid to be put to the test, since you might discover you are not indispensable? Or might you be a Timid Soul, anxious to have peace at any price and afraid to make your siblings angry with you and perhaps even unwilling to go to see your parents? Or are you inclined to let things drift, so that out of sheer inertia you fail to approach your brothers or sisters?

Honest answers to such honest self-questioning may free you to give your siblings a chance, and more than a chance, to share in your job. Even if no suggestions or offers to help have ever come spontaneously from them, you are likely to get an agreeable surprise from their favorable response to your invitation or request to help in making and executing plans for your parents' benefit. Social agencies are often told of relatives, "There's no use even asking him—he won't do a thing"; yet when such relatives are approached, the agencies' experience has usually been to find them quite co-operative.

In the good old democratic way, hold a family council where everyone can air his views, share opinions, and jointly consider plans. If one of your siblings has died and there is a surviving in-law, be sure to invite him or her. A strong attachment between aging persons and the husband or wife of a beloved deceased child is not unusual and such in-laws may remain a firm, helpful part of the family unit.

Once your generation has had its conclave, your parents should be in on further discussion. The experience of meeting together and talking things over can be richly satisfying to all of you. Just as you were a family twenty or thirty or forty years ago, so are you a family now. And so will you be twenty or thirty or forty years hence, with you who are now concerned about the elderly being yourselves the elderly, and another generation, let us hope, concerned about you.

Unless your mother or father has an adequate income, doubtless there will have to be some talking about support. Naturally those siblings who are best off will be able to contribute the largest amounts. Others may be able to provide in shelter or service what they cannot in cash, to the end that all may take part in the present stage of family experience.

Income tax exemption is another part of the financial picture which ought to be considered. If a parent is completely dependent on you, you get a six hundred dollar exemption when he is under sixty-five and double exemption if he is over that age. If he is not entirely dependent but you pay over half of his support, you are allowed his exemption. However, you must declare his reportable income. If your siblings share in total or partial support, you may divide the exemption among you. It might be advisable to share it every year, or it might work out better to take turns with it from year to year. Much depends on each child's proportionate contribution to support and the tax bracket he or she is in. But whatever taxes, large or small, are involved, get expert advice from a lawyer or tax consultant.

As a rule, too, the personnel of the Internal Revenue Service in your district are helpful in giving information on such matters as allowable deductions and what part of your parent's income, if any, such as that from social security, is not reportable. After you have conferred with the expert, you and your brothers and sisters have a sound basis for agreement on what deductions are fair, considering each one's human obligations and financial resources.

The question of where your parents are going to live is also a matter for sibling discussion. As we have already pointed out in Chapter 2, the decision should reach a balance between what is best for the older generation and most feasible for the younger. If it is not possible for your parents to remain by themselves or to be in group care, it may well be that one of the siblings can easily move in with them. Or your parents may clearly fit better into one of your homes than into any of the others. Do not be misled by preconceptions that "comfort," "service," and the opportunity "to take things easy" will spell certain happiness for old people, and therefore almost routinely settle upon the home of the son or daughter who has most space, most money, or domestic help. Considerations we have mentioned before such as urban versus rural surroundings, presence or absence of young children, the chance to feel useful, and congeniality in ways of life are vital. It cannot be said too often that there is no formula for the best adjustment of an aging parent and the son's or daughter's family with whom he lives; good results can be obtained only through careful calculation of individual differences. About the only categorical "absolutely not" is any such deal as "You take Dad and I'll take Mom." The separation of couples who for many years have lived congenially together, a cruel practice in some old people's homes, is certainly nothing to be imitated by children.

Since in this general section we are talking about you and your parents living together, we are going on the assumption that the consensus of the council of siblings is, first, that your parents should move in with one of their children, and second, that your home is selected as most suitable. Now you can go on to make arrangements with your siblings to have your parents with them some part of the time.

For your parents, spending time with the others not only gives the advantage of change of scene but also of not being exclusively and narrowingly attached to one family. For you and your family, there is the slight disadvantage of having to make afresh all the readjustments described in Chapter 10 each time your mother or father returns from a visit. But this drawback is outweighed by the benefit of you and your family having some periods of privacy when you can be all by yourselves.

Be sure that no matter how frequent or prolonged your parents' stays with your siblings may be, it is quite clear that your home is "home." It is dreary to be a chronic guest. "Home" is the place where you keep any possessions not taken along on journeys. Its address is the one given to the post office as "permanent" and stated when documents must be signed. It establishes voting residence. There is all the difference in the world between "I live with my son (or daughter) in Boonestown," and "I spend part of the year with each of my children," even though actual apportionment of time among siblings may be identical. Old or young, anyone who feels transient is liable to feel dispossessed, and the dispossessed take little interest in the affairs of any community. Those who have a sense of roots, on the other hand, can without age limit play a part in what is going on in the neighborhood, town, county, or city. Your parent, in short, though he may visit a sibling for as long as "The Man Who Came to Dinner," should never be in any doubt that his anchorage, his base, is with you.

Likewise, no aging parent ought ever to feel that his children are parceling out his time among them as a grim duty. Unfortunately, too many old folks are treated like Mrs. Appleton, who spent exactly three months every year with each of her four children. "I have to have Mother next," preceded the visits. Of course the old lady did not overhear such remarks, but their spirit came through and she could not but know that she was shunted from one child to another.

The Gray family handled "taking turns with Mother" much better. The dates of the beginnings and ends of her fairly regular stays with each of her children were not rigidly set; insofar as it was feasible, she was the one who planned the timing of her respective visits. Also, no one ever "took" her from one sibling's home to another's; someone from the next place she was to go would "come to get" her. Instead of a periodic feeling that her children were making sure they would get rid of her, therefore, she enjoyed the heart-warming implication, "We can't wait to see you."

Generally, when you work out where and when Mother or Father is to visit, avoid decisions based on clichés as consistently as in planning with whom they live. For example, the fact that travel folders play up North for summer and South for winter may have absolutely no bearing on what your parents want. If Mom and Dad were born and bred in Massachusetts and love snow, you do them no favor to insist that they spend the winter months with brother Jack who lives in Southern California.

When it comes to celebration of holidays, there is also no rule applicable to all old folks. Some families make Thanksgiving the big occasion for get-togethers; some Christmas. Your parent may like the feeling of having all the children and grandchildren assemble at your home, which now is also his or hers, or then again they may prefer to make holidays the occasion for going somewhere else.

All such means of encouraging your parents to exercise options, however minor, are to the good, for they help to lessen feelings of dependence. Also important for preserving the spirit of independence are the opportunities your mother and father have to do as they like with money.

12

DOLLARS AND SENSE

MONEY IS ONE OF the things most of us are least willing to discuss, although—like some other unmentionables—it has a tremendous influence on personal and family happiness. A strange coyness seems to come over many people when questions of how much and how it is to be obtained need to be discussed with those nearest and dearest to them, as if the very mention of ways and means would turn the bright gold of affection into sordid dross. Other people actually don't realize how important money is to all of us. It is the medium of exchange in our civilization, what we have to have in order to get anything we want. Everyone needs it if he is to carry on.

Since your parents are not living where they can get along by barter or with wampum they are no exception, so the more frankly you recognize the great significance of money in their lives, the better you will be able to do your job. Make up your mind that it is neither indelicate nor crude to discuss money with them and everyone intimately concerned with them, and then proceed to have clear understandings about their source and use of funds.

An aging widow especially, but quite possibly an aging man, too, may welcome children's advice on financial matters. If your parents seek your advice, go over with them what assets they have, such as a house, car, savings account, stocks or bonds, and also what liabilities, such as a mortgage or other loan. Look into the possible redemption of life insurance policies, collection of endowment policies, and, if desirable, cash for matured bonds; check on the receipt of annuities or pensions—industrial, military, or governmental.

If they have been making social security payments, be sure that they get all the benefits from OASDI (Old Age and Survivors Disability Insurance) to which they are entitled. These do not come automatically as a kind of sixty-second birthday present or larger one at sixty-five; they have been earned, and they have to be claimed. In order for your parent to learn what benefits, if any, he may get, he should apply at the local Social Security Administration office, complete with his social security number and birth certificate or other evidence of his age. If there is difficulty locating it through the telephone directory, the post office will supply the address. Should neither he nor you be able to apply in person for his OASDI benefits, telephone or write or get someone to telephone for you. If your parent has lost his social security number, essential for collecting anything on what he has been paying under that number, you will find your local Social Security Administration office helpful in advising what steps need to be taken in order to get re-identification from national headquarters, Social Security Administration, Baltimore, Md. 21235.

Don't overlook that S in OASDI. Your widowed mother may not be collecting the share of your late father's social security income to which she is entitled. Indeed, under certain circumstances you yourself might be entitled to some. In any case, as many families do not realize, there is an OASDI allowance for burial expenses. (For disability benefits under social security provisions, see Chapter 24.)

So intricate and complex are social security regulations that we shall not attempt to set forth the ifs, ands, and buts determining whether and how much an individual can collect. Our best advice is to find out from the local Social Security Administration office. Very seldom would it be necessary to call in a lawyer to insure that your parent gets his just deserts. If it is, and you cannot afford a competent private-practice attorney's fees, in most cities you can apply to an eleemosynary Legal Aid Society or the local Bar Association referral service, through which the community's most able lawyers give limited service for nominal fees.

If your parent is without funds, he might be eligible for Old Age Assistance (OAA). This is not the same as OASDI. OASDI is paid-up insurance, OAA is allotted by the Department of Welfare. When your parent was young he probably thought of people receiving public funds for their support as "on relief" and may feel that for him to receive OAA is a "disgrace." Try to disabuse him of this idea by explaining that over the years his contributions to society have earned him the right to have society make some contribution to him. If he lives with you it is likely to make him feel good if you permit him to use some of his OAA allowance toward his board. The amount paid by OAA varies widely among the states and so do "relative responsibility" laws. In some, your parent is not eligible for OAA if any children or perhaps even grandchildren or other relatives are able to help with his support. In others, relatives' means are not taken into consideration, only the financial situation of the old person himself. Your local or state Department of Welfare will give you the facts.

Should your parents have some capital funds and request your help, plan with them how best to invest these. Whether their money should be put into, or remain in a savings account, federal savings and loan association, bonds, mortgages, stocks, real property, or various combinations of these will depend very largely on how much they have and whether they can afford to take even mild risks for the sake of more return on their money. If you knew exactly how long your mother or father were going to live, management of their money would be relatively simple, because then they could just merrily draw down their capital so much a year.

Money management for those along in years is such an individual matter that unless you are well versed in finance, go to a lawyer or banker for advice. Many insurance agents and brokers, and stockbrokers, also give excellent financial advice, but since they earn their living on commissions, they would be superhuman if they had no bias. Investment counselors make nothing out of buying or selling but work on the basis of a small percentage of the funds they hopefully make grow. Generally investment counselors will not manage funds of less than $100,000, but there are exceptions.

Despite the World War II bond campaigns which made millions of Americans security conscious for the first time, and the mutual funds and investment trusts pitched to small investors, many people still seem to think that carefully planned investments are something only for the rich, and that "a balanced portfolio," "inflationary and deflationary trends," or the difference between stocks and bonds has nothing to do with ordinary folks. But even if your parents have no more than a thousand dollars which they do not need to use in the very near future, it might as well be working for them. Indeed, the income a small investor draws from a small amount of money may be more important to him than the income a large investor draws from a large one.

Similarly, no matter how large or small your parent's estate, you ought to urge him to have a will drawn by a lawyer. Do not let any embarrassment of seeming to be grabbing something for yourself deter you from helping your parent to will what he owns to whom he wishes. With a properly drawn will he will have the satisfaction of knowing that his favorite clock will become the property of his favorite grandson or that his books will be owned by someone who really appreciates them. Without a legally phrased and witnessed will, his property, because of various state laws governing inheritance when there is no will, may go to the persons whom he would least want to have it. Moreover, an expertly worded will can often save costly administration expenses, not to mention family fights likely to be the last kind of situation your parent would like to have result from his death. It is also advisable for your parent to consult a lawyer in connection with any health insurance policy he considers taking out after he is sixty-five. Some such policies offer no protection against the very diseases and conditions from which an older person is most likely to suffer. A few are outright rackets to exploit the elderly.

No matter how much confidence your parents have in your wisdom and integrity, and though you may be told, "Don't worry me with details," it is not a good idea to assume a "leave it all to me" attitude and keep them entirely in the dark about their finances. Even with full power to use your own judgment, inform your mother or father periodically as to how much they currently have and at least in a general way what investments they have.

Broadly, the expenses of your parents' care come under two categories. The first includes such fundamentals as food, shelter, and routine medical care. Barring acute illness or other emergencies, these costs will be pretty much fixed by your own scale of living and the general state of your parents' health. For purposes of this discussion, we shall call them "living" expenses.

The second category of costs takes in clothing, entertainment, grooming, carfare, tobacco, gifts, and contributions—as, for example, to church. Though some of these items, such as clothing to cover nakedness, are as essential as any under the first classification, they are all more flexible; clothing, for instance, can vary widely in quality and amount. We shall call this second general kind of expenses "personal."

What goes out must come in, and your parents will either have or not have money of their own. Let us assume first that they have an income comfortable enough to cover both living and personal expenses. In that case, all you need to do is to decide with them how much board they should pay.

Some sons and daughters are sentimentally reluctant to "take anything" from aging parents. But if your mother and father are perfectly well able to pay their way in your home, let them do so as a sturdy prop to independence, and accept their regular contributions as unprotestingly and unemotionally as if they came from a stranger.

Even if your parents have an income relatively smaller than yours, as long as it is sufficient to cover personal and some living expenses it is good for them to pay board. Though they may not possibly be able to cover their maintenance in a home run on the scale of yours, do what you can to let them feel that they are carrying their weight. The prosperous Murdocks, who lived in an eight-room house staffed by a couple, handled such a situation well. Murdock, Sr., before he came to live in two of the rooms, had been getting along modestly in a tiny apartment with the services of a weekly cleaning woman. When he asked his son somewhat apprehensively how much would cover the cost of maintaining him because "I'm not ready yet to sponge on you," Murdock, Jr. answered casually, "Oh, just about what it cost you to live by yourself." It is not too difficult to keep older people satisfied that they are really paying their way, because most of us base our estimates of household costs on what we have been used to spending in our own homes.

Whether your parents' income is small or large, once they have paid whatever is agreed upon for living expenses, what they do with the rest of it is their business. Unless you must take legal steps to have your mother or father declared incompetent (see Chapter 25), you have no right to go beyond a suggestion as to what they do with their own money. Grandpa may give the children absurdly extravagant presents; Grandma may ridiculously overtip. You may think they use poor judgment, but don't be like Ellen Jones. She scolded and criticized her eighty-six-year-old mother for buying a new, expensive fur coat and confided to her friends, "Of all the crazy things to do! She'll never get the wear out of it." Ellen, in effect, was announcing the fact that she was afraid Mama would run through all her money and leave nothing for Ellen.

Now let's assume that your parents have some income or capital, but so little that it can't be stretched for both categories of expenditures. Which way will they feel less dependent—if they cover their basic living expenses by paying board and are given what they need for personal expenditures, or if you provide their living and they keep their own money for such clothing and incidentals as they wish?

There isn't the slightest doubt as to the answer: under the second arrangement your parents will be happier. Somehow it comes easier to all of us to pay for our own movies, even though someone else buys our food, than it does the other way round. Somehow the worst part of being broke isn't having our friends help out with the rent, but not being able to buy gifts for, perhaps, those very same friends. None of this is logical, but it's so. Carry the fixed living expenses for your parents, therefore, and leave them free to use their own limited funds at their own pleasure and rate.

In the bottom of their hearts, to be sure, they will know that you are supporting them and that they are not really independent. But there are fewer reminders of dependence in the meals they eat at your table, the fuel that warms their rooms, the doctors' bills you quietly pay, or the sheets you buy for their bed than there would be in cigarettes, ice-cream sodas, an occasional taxi, a magazine or any other incidental outlay, however small, which might be regarded as a personal indulgence.

But suppose that, like many elderly men and women, your parents are left with no money at all of their own. In that case there is no question about who covers living expenses: it must, of course, be the children.

Unfortunately, many a family which cheerfully and generously enough provides for its old people's maintenance almost completely overlooks provision of the wherewithal for personal outlays which can make the difference between living and existing.

It is years, for instance, since old Mrs. Gorman has had a new dress. Like most old people she isn't hard on her clothes. Also, like most who are conscious of their dependence, she tries to make what she has last. Her children assume correctly enough, "Mother doesn't go anywhere." It never seems to occur to them that new clothes give a lift to any woman, old or young, or that if Mother had more clothes she might feel like going more places.

Mr. Mason's children are equally thoughtless. Though he is well housed and well fed in a daughter's home, nobody gives thought to the fact that he might like to buy a friend a glass of beer once in a while, might want to remember his grandchildren's birthdays with presents, might enjoy going out and buying his own cigarettes more than taking them from the box which stands always filled on the coffee table.

Make sure that your parents have some money which is all their own, to use exactly as they please. Indeed, allow them to treat you with it once in a while; this is the surest proof that the money, though it may be given them, is really theirs. It doesn't matter what you call it—pocket money, pin money, spending money, drawing account, or allowance—as long as it has no strings. Actually it is a salary, a salary for the past.

The amount your parents have for personal expenses, decided upon at a family council and later discussed with them, should be based realistically on their needs and your ability to pay when you take into account the needs of other people who may be dependent on you, like your children. As in the bathroom occupancy we discussed in Chapter 10, neither one generation nor another ought to be called upon to make all the sacrifices. On the one hand if your popular daughter Louisa needs a new formal, this should be taken into account when you figure for your mother's wardrobe. But on the other, Grandma ought not to have to wear the same threadbare winter coat for the fifth year because Louisa howls that she just couldn't be caught dead in last year's ski outfit. Remember always that with money, as with other elements of life, you are dealing not merely with so many individuals but with a family unit. Apportionment of funds, therefore, like that of space and time, needs to be calculated so that it can best serve all of your interests and pursuits.

Some people of any age are impractical about spending money, and no matter what they have are incapable of stretching it to supply their needs. Your father may spread himself as Santa Claus and then, in January, be without a wearable heavy overcoat. Your mother may be so addicted to movies and treats for her friends that she may have nothing left to supply herself with stockings. Of course you can't let your parents go without necessities, so you will have to see that they get what they don't get for themselves. Figure, rather, on a lesser allowance in the first place, so that you can afford to supplement it with essential extras. Another way you can fill holes that aren't or can't be filled by regular pocket money is through gifts. There are always birthdays, and Christmas, when clothing is acceptable even to proudly independent individuals.

Your parents may be among the older men and women who find it profoundly embarrassing to accept cash. If so, you might see that their funds for personal expenses are mailed or put for them in a checking account.

An occasional old person won't accept an allowance from his children in any form. If your parent is one of these, you might make the "salary" a real one in the form of payment for present services—Father perhaps can earn by trimming the hedge, Mother by baby-sitting.

You may find it hard to accept the idea of "pay" to your parents for doing anything for you. They will probably find it even harder to take being paid for services they'd like to give out of love. You will need to have a frank discussion with them on the matter, a free and considerate exchange of thoughts. From your viewpoint, tell them that the service is valuable to you and that you would have to pay anyone else to perform it.

Mrs. Poole and her mother-in-law, after a rather poor start when the older woman moved into her son's and daughter-in-law's home, arrived at a mutually satisfactory salary arrangement. For weeks the destitute old lady, who had been used to working hard all her life, sat about idle and forlorn in her new home while the younger woman, busy enough for two with a part-time job, the care of a sizable house and two school-age children, dropped exhausted into bed each night. Mrs. Poole, Sr. wanted to offer to help, but felt she might be interfering or implying that her daughter-in-law wasn't competent. Mrs. Poole, Jr. was dying to have her mother-in-law help, but didn't like to seem exploiting. One day, while Mrs. Poole, Jr., was at work, the older woman baked an apple pie and produced it with apologies—"I didn't think you'd mind." Far from minding, Mrs. Poole, Jr., was delighted not to have to make dessert that night but, fearful of letting her mother-in-law think she wanted to press her into service, was no more than politely grateful. A few weeks later, with even more profuse apologies, Mrs. Poole, Sr. greeted her daughter-in-law on her arrival home with the news that she had done her washing. "I was just fascinated by your machine and wanted to try it," she remarked timorously.

Mrs. Poole, Jr. had a brainstorm. "Listen!" she said. "From now on I'm going to pay you regularly for work you do in the house. I'd have to pay someone else, and she wouldn't do it as well."

Mrs. Poole, Sr. protested, "You're doing enough, giving me my living," but the younger woman was firm. And so they embarked on a well-thought-through arrangement in which everyone in the household had certain duties, with Granny earning a salary for the substantial contributions she made.

Mrs. Poole, Sr. became the happiest old woman in the neighborhood. "The neighbors talk," she chuckled. "They say, 'It's a shame to see you doing all that work.' But I love it!" And the first time she treated the whole family to dinner in a restaurant on her pay, she was radiant.

For Mrs. Poole, Jr., too, the arrangement worked out well. She no longer felt hesitant about accepting such help as her mother-in-law could reasonably give her, and she was released from so many domestic duties that she was able to advance in her job. Every time she got a raise in pay, Granny's pay went up too. Granny protested, but she was told with truth, "If you weren't helping, I wouldn't be able to earn this much."

Unfortunately none of the devices for helping your financially dependent parents to preserve some feeling of independence will work out if control of funds is in the hands of one of those individuals who so much needs to have a feeling of power that he must be asked for every penny he doles out. This kind of person will make a big theoretical point of acting in the old folks' protection when he hands out dollars and cents in dribbles and only for specific purchases about which he is duly informed. If you can possibly manage it, avoid letting him handle money for your parents. If you are not the only one in the family who contributes to their support, perhaps you can arrange with your siblings to set up a checking account in your mother's or father's name. The main thing never to forget is that to be able to say and feel, "It's mine, all mine," is as inspiriting at sixty or seventy or eighty or ninety as at any other time of life.

And this goes not only for money that can be spent, but also for things that can be possessed.

13

THEIR BELONGINGS

Theoretically we are not supposed to find material things important: we should feel that what counts is not what we possess but character; not what can be seen and touched, but spiritual intangibles. Few of us in actuality, however, can be like members of religious orders and renounce worldly goods. Mundane as it may seem, the ordinary human being who has nothing not only feels like nothing but also is nothing in the eyes of others. Even if your parents have to give up living by themselves, therefore, make sure that they keep some belongings of their own. Strip them of everything they have accumulated over the years, and you tear away associations with a once full, productive life. This is the ruthless equivalent of the primitive custom of leaving the aged in the open to die.

Sometimes old people, in a dramatic admission of dependence, sign or give away everything they own. Or an assortment of relatives and children may put more or less subtle pressure upon them to do so. An easy, inexpensive way to get odds and ends of household goods you've always wanted is to say, "You're not going to need that dinner set any more," or "There'll never be room for that chest of drawers in Harold's house." It is a wise child who intervenes to protect his parents from their own impulse to strip themselves, or from human vultures who gather around dying independence. The old folks are not going to move into their new home with you for only a week or two before they die. They are embarking on a new phase of life, which will be happier, more comfortable, and more satisfying if, in their bedroom at any rate, they are surrounded by things of their own.

The older a person grows, the more meaningful and important grow the familiar bed or the familiar chair. So to reinforce your parent's feeling, "This is really my home," his own room ought to be furnished with his own well-known possessions—furniture, books, family pictures, clocks, vases, or anything he wants.

Even if good sense is on your side, let him have his way in his personal living space. From your viewpoint, for instance, it is utterly absurd to ship that old hair mattress of his from Wisconsin, where he has always lived, to Florida where he is going to live with you. For one thing, from sad experience you know that about the only sure way to prevent malodorous mildew from ruining mattresses is to use foam rubber ones with ticking especially treated for the tropics. For another, you could buy him a lovely, comfortable new mattress at little, if any more than the cost of shipping that lumpy old thing. But your parent may date from a time when hair mattresses were the finest available and a kind of status symbol in contrast to felt; he spread himself to get this one which, he was assured, with occasional redoing would "last for life"; and he feels homey and relaxed lying on it. Or, the bone of contention may be your mother's beaten-up woolen afghan which had been knitted for her by her deceased sister Lucy, and for which you would like to substitute an equally warm synthetic coverlet. Having lived all her previous life below the Mason-Dixon line where moths are not much of a problem, Mom does not realize the production it is, in your apartment, in New York City to have woolen articles cleaned, moth-proofed and stored during the summer.

One way to avoid continual irritation for yourself and at the same time satisfy your parent's emotional need for "a bunch of junk" or "clutter" is to let him decide when and how to clean his own room and, if he is physically able to care for it, to make its maintenance his responsibility. Although he may not always remember to do so, if you ask him to keep the door of his room closed, this may help you to endure his personal housekeeping. Try to be as understanding as the Welfare Department of a small Wyoming city, which humanely permitted a one-hundred-five-year-old Negro, a former slave who proudly displayed his emancipation paper signed by Abraham Lincoln, to continue living all by himself as he wished in an appallingly disordered one-room shack, although a bed was available for him in a good nursing home.

Often a daughter or daughter-in-law does not deprive an elderly person of the things he wants to keep to spare herself trouble, but out of mistaken kindness and generosity. "Dad had an old golden oak desk that was an eyesore," Mrs. Ogden told her friends, "so I got rid of it and bought him a nice new secretary instead." She did not add, nor did she realize, that along with the cast-off desk went a lifetime of memories. Long ago at that desk, a young man had studied nights to get ahead in the world. Later a father had helped his children there with homework. Still later its pigeonholes had been filled with the papers of a successful businessman.

Mrs. Myers, who likewise had the best intentions in the world, induced her mother-in-law to get rid of her thirty-five-year-old cheap bedroom furniture and be "treated" to everything brand new. The decorator who had planned the rest of the Myers' attractive suburban home recommended, as appropriate for an old lady, colonial mahogany furniture and a color scheme of lavender accented with green. A day bed converted the big sunny room into a sitting room, and altogether it was a *House Beautiful* dream. But unfortunately, though Mrs. Myers, Sr. was politely grateful for the generosity that prompted the decorating, she never felt at home with her new period-and-pastel elegance, as she had with her big old double bed and the overstuffed chair.

It may be that your parents' possessions, far from being ordinary or shabby, are fine and handsome; heirlooms or purchased, they may indeed be better than anything of your own. Your parents may be quite insistent that you "take these lovely things," or "use this in place of what you have, you'll never be able to get anything so good." But except for what goes into their own quarters, do not give house room to anything you do not really want. It may hurt your mother's and father's feelings to have their beautiful dining room suite knocked down at auction, but if you find it more convenient to eat in a dinette there is no reason to convert your living room to accommodate a table seating twelve. Your mother and father need to bring with them enough of their own belongings to make them feel at home, but not so many that you will be swamped. As in everything else connected with doubling up, both generations will have to give up something—but for neither generation must or should this be all or nothing.

You may be reproached with insensitive lack of appreciation for the beauty and value of old things. You may feel downright mean when your mother, with tears in her eyes, begs you to reconsider taking the grandfather's clock—which won't fit in your small, low-ceilinged hall without blocking off the door of the coat closet. But if you allow yourself to be loaded with objects inappropriate to your home or manner of living, you put yourself and your family under as much psychological unease as you might put your parents if, in their quarters, you forced upon them streamlined Danish modern furniture and brilliantly colored, abstract-patterned draperies. A temporary period of strain, regrets, and perhaps even arguments are better for all of you than the long pull of living together constantly impeded by your not being relaxed and at home in your own home.

Some older women have virtually made a career of being nurse-maids to things, and if your mother was one of these in her own home there is another hazard in your taking in too many of your parents' possessions. Mrs. Singleton, who moved into her daughter's home along with a large conglomeration of mediocre Oriental rugs, silverware, good and poor paintings, tapestry chairs, and lamps carved out of semiprecious stones, takes the attitude: "This is my valuable furniture—now it's up to you to look after it, and well!" Entirely overlooking the fact that she had kept house with a staff of servants and that her daughter has none, Mrs. Singleton expects the silver to be polished weekly with a special polish and a special cloth, the lamps tenderly sponged in every crevice, and the rugs taken out into the yard to be beaten. With three young children tracking mud into the house, the daughter surreptitiously vacuums the rugs when her mother is out, but aside from this defection rather than be continually reproached and criticized, she slaves over her mother's possessions. Although Mrs. Singleton's attitude toward her things may be extreme, in nearly every family the psychological value of possessions for the older generation needs to be weighed against the burden of their care for the younger.

Some older people are just as much interested in accumulating as younger ones, and within reason and the space limitations of your home, your parents ought not to be discouraged from acquiring new things. Your mother or father may enjoy getting more books, changing decorations for their bedroom, or adding to a collection of stamps or coins.

Whenever an elderly person moves out of the place he has been occupying, the question arises "What shall be done with the things he doesn't take along?" Whether to distribute certain possessions among the family, to give them to charity, or to sell them is an individual matter that each family has to decide for itself in a council of siblings and parents. Many articles have appeared in popular magazines about the treasures in attics, the unsuspected wealth buried in Aunt Jemima's old trunk, or the priceless yellowed newspapers that have been piled up for years in basements, but usually what seem to be first editions turn out to be worthless second editions, and at the time that you go to sell pine, you are told that cherry is the only thing that brings good prices—or vice versa. So the less you count on your parents' cashing in on what they have, the less you will be disappointed, and if anything does turn out to have real value it will be a pleasant surprise.

In any case, if there is anything of your parents' you or one of your siblings especially wants now, offer to buy it rather than suggest that it be willed to you.

When it comes to possessions more personal than furniture, such as jewelry, the same principles apply. Your parents ought not to divest themselves. If your mother says in offering you a lace scarf or a brooch, "I won't be needing this any more," your acceptance of the gift is like answering, "I agree, you're through with living." This is often the first evidence of despondency and depression and rather than acting as a reinforcement you would do well to get psychiatric consultation. Even more forthrightly, your parent may remark, "Take it, I won't be around much longer." Implicit in your receiving what is thus offered is your concurrence, "You're right, you'll soon be dead."

Some children take the initiative in acquiring their parents' possessions either by frankly asking for them or, more indirectly, by asking that they be loaned—with no intention of return. But when a person is left with nothing at all either to will or to give away, it not only does something unfortunate to him; it also creates an undesirable reaction in his children. Somehow or other, if Pop still holds a deed to real property in his name his wishes concerning it are still respected, but once it is turned over to his son, remodeling or a grand slashing down of trees is no longer considered Pop's concern.

No old person, in short, ought to feel or be made to feel that he must give up everything in order to be cared for by his children, as a public assistance client must show destitution in order to be eligible to receive funds. If your parent parts with everything material he loses even more than possessions that might be pawned. What he turns over to another generation is a segment of life itself, which no one should rightly renounce until he is dead.

And since inanimate objects with which there are associations have so much meaning for older people, it is no wonder that human beings who can share memories have even more.

14

THEIR FRIENDS—AND YOURS

As PEOPLE GROW OLDER they are liable to lose many things that were formerly the very stuff of their lives, such as their own home, their family's need of them, and their work. The more these drop away, the more the old friends who went along with them through various stages of youth and maturity attain a special importance. Almost uniquely, when lives have run parallel there is a kind of precious continuity in experience. It is not even shared by individuals dear as a husband or wife, who as a rule come later upon the scene, nor by one's children, who change with striking, apparent rapidity from infants into adults.

Even the sight of contemporaries' aging holds a kind of reassurance. When someone exclaims, "My, how Bill shows his age!" or "Hasn't Martha grown gray!" rarely is there the saddening thought, "I must be getting old, too, because they are." Rather, back of the speaker's mind, is something like "I look younger."

As part of your job, encourage and help your parents to keep up with their friends. There is comfort and sustenance for older people in association with those who have lived and suffered and rejoiced through the same phases of life and history as they; whose experiences as young folks or young marrieds or young parents or middle-aged men and women took place at the same time as theirs; who have common memories of the Battle of Manila or Armistice Day or the beginning of stardom for now-aging actors and actresses. In giving up their own home and moving in with you, your parents are at best like a tree transplanted. As in an old plant, the roots in an old person go very deep, and none more deeply than those of old friendships. So if these are cut, the shock can be severe.

Your parent may not be fully aware of how important his old friends can be to his emotional survival. Indeed, when he first comes to live with you, you might have a good deal of difficulty in getting him to keep up with them. He may act indifferent about "seeing anybody outside the family." Or he may even state expressly, firmly, and perhaps disagreeably, that he doesn't want to go with former intimates. For such an attitude there may be any one of several causes. Your mother or father may feel like a kind of permanent guest in your home and wanting to be a good guest, may be reluctant to presume on your hospitality by receiving friends. Or they may sink into the idea "I'm on the shelf now; I have no right to my friends because I'm living with John and Mary." Or they may think that their cronies are too old to behave suitably in younger people's homes.

Or, like Mrs. Rossiter, they may shrink from previous contacts because they feel they have lost face by becoming dependent. Although in her younger years she was an exceedingly sociable woman, at seventy she rejected old friendships. So keenly did she feel the "disgrace" of being in what she genteelly called "reduced circumstances" and having to move in with her daughter that she refused every invitation because, she said plaintively, "I have no way to reciprocate now." The daughter let matters go with an occasional, ineffectual "Now don't be foolish, Mother," or "Why don't you dine there anyway?" and within a few years Mrs. Rossiter's friends grew tired of making one-sided advances and getting consistent rebuffs. The telephone stopped ringing for Mrs. Rossiter and the postman brought very few letters. Long before she died, Mrs. Rossiter had changed from an attractive, vivacious woman into a spiritless burden and bore to herself and the family with whom she lived.

Even if your parent's attitude is not as extreme as Mrs. Rossiter's you may have to use all your ingenuity to preserve the ties of old friendships. The first stages of adjustment to living with one's children are the hardest, and if you let an initial tendency toward being a hermit go unchecked, you will both regret it later. For a while, at least, you will probably have to take the social initiative for your mother or father.

In addition to making room in your house or apartment for them, make room for their friends. Of course it will involve some inconvenience and trouble if you arrange for them to give tea or card parties or lend your home for church groups or club meetings. But in the long run, helping your parents to have some social life of their own will pay off for you as well as for them. You won't always have to be worrying about taking Mother along to the movies or Father down to the beach because the poor things have nothing else to do. Also, and more important, they are likely to be more cheerful and easier to live with if they have a lively give-and-take with their friends than if they sink into social stagnation.

It is not necessary nor even desirable, however, that you be about when your parents entertain. There is no reason why their pals must also be yours. In the days when you and your mother and father were younger, the chances are that each of you was bored by the other's friends, and since you are still members of different generations the situation will not have changed. When your parents' company comes to your home, behave with them as well-bred youngsters in well-run households are taught to behave with their parents' guests; that is, greet the visitors pleasantly, sit with them for a few minutes, and then take yourself off. Once in a while you might, indeed, let your parents have the place to themselves when they give a party.

One of the greatest causes of unpleasantness in the home where Mrs. Oliver lived with her son and daughter-in-law was the old lady's insistence that they be present whenever she had company. Supinely, they gave in "not to hurt Mother" and suffered through evening after evening of petty gossip in which they did not have the slightest interest. But the appeasement failed. Mrs. Oliver complained continually that Joe and Mabel looked bored, didn't contribute sufficiently to the conversation, failed to give her friends proper respect. To avoid similar situations which make nobody happy, make it clear to your parents from the beginning that their friends are theirs. It may be painful to settle this question but not nearly so painful as years and years in which you will feel victimized and your parent unsatisfied.

If your mother and father have come from another community to live with you, be sure that now and then they can return to their old home to visit lifelong friends. It may be as important, or more important, for them to do this than to visit members of the family. Correspondence is another way for them to maintain old ties. If they are handicapped by failing eyesight or hands too trembling or crippled by arthritis to make letter writing simple, your children might take turns doing it for them. Or, like David Krauss, who had nothing wrong with his vision and coordination but who found writing longhand letters a distasteful chore, they might learn typing as he did—at seventy-two.

Perhaps one by one your parent's contemporaries will die off, and he or she will become almost the sole survivor of an entire social group. Fortunately the loss of old friends is not as devastating to the aged as one might expect when few are left. Yet although death as something occurring in the normal course of events seems to be more acceptable to older than to younger folk, it still has significance, and among certain kinds of people, going to funerals has enormous importance. Do your best to make it possible for your parent to attend any and every funeral he wishes.

Whether or not your parents have old friends, help them to make new ones. Never mind if your mother or father says, "But I'm too old to make new friends" or "At my age you can't start taking up with strangers." Such commonly held notions contain only a germ of truth. The fact of the matter is that it is not so hard to make new friends when one is aging as it is to make the moves to make the friends. If, therefore, you make some of such moves for your parents, whether sixty or seventy, they can still experience the joys of fresh, stimulating contacts.

In helping to establish these for your mother or father, remember that almost any enjoyed pursuit—card playing, volunteer work in connection with a church or social agency, the movies, bird watching, reading, or watching television—can be the link with like-minded men or women of any age. Besides such stereotyped hobbies as handcrafts or collecting, there is a wide range of interests—highbrow, middlebrow and lowbrow—which makes people congenial. Since you probably won't be able to depend on your parent to take the initiative in searching out kindred spirits, take it upon yourself, never forgetting to aim not at what *you* like or would like your parent to like, but what he or she actually does like.

Though you may have to look hard and diligently for individuals or a group with whom your mother or father will fit in friendship, by drawing them into a social circle of their own you will be making yourself freer in yours. Nearly all of us, no matter what our age, want to be with people and feel a part of something. An aging person, especially, needs reassurance that he isn't totally "out of things" and if he doesn't get it in one way, you may be sure he will in another. Many an old man or woman who wants to be in the center of everything is simply people-hungry, and with enough personal social outlets, wouldn't be so interfering, attention-seeking, and floor-holding at gatherings of another generation's friends.

No one can tell you exactly what social maneuvers to make, for much depends on your personality and your parent's and on the way you live. But what some resourceful sons and daughters have accomplished may be suggestive.

Mrs. Randolph King, instead of letting the community know about her mother-in-law's coming to live with her with the usual resigned announcement after the fact, made the elder lady's arrival a gala occasion. In advance, she had sent out invitations for a party "to meet Mrs. Jasper King." Unless you live in so small and tight-knit a community that any invitation to meet anyone would be absurd, you too can festively introduce a parent by way of anything from a formal reception complete with catering to a beer-and-sandwich evening.

Ernestine Pratt, a professor of mathematics, virtually created a group of which her mother, Mrs. Dodd, could become part, although the elder lady had interests quite different from her daughter's. All her life she had been a housewife, concerned with the kitchen and garden. Wisely, Mrs. Pratt did not expect her mother suddenly to become interested in differential calculus and the Einstein theory, but sought out people in the community who might enjoy discussing recipes and the best way to make compost. It was relatively simple to locate a garden club, which she soon induced her mother to join. But to get her with congenial cooks was more difficult. Young housewives were too involved to devote much time to virtuoso cookery, while most older women said they "just didn't care any more." With persistence, however, Mrs. Pratt, offering her own kitchen as the first experimental center, managed to assemble a handful of middle-aged and elderly women interested in exchanging recipes and comparing techniques. They soon organized, electing Mrs. Dodd their first president, and within a year the "Cookery

Clique" was a going and growing club. Mrs. Dodd was not the only one delighted with the activity. "You've helped to give me a new lease on domestic life," one member gratefully told Mrs. Pratt, and another, "Belonging to this club has lifted my cooking from a routine chore to a sport."

A businessman, Horace Rand, helped his retired businessman father to see new faces and make new friends. He invited the older man to some Rotary Club luncheons and took him along to an occasional out-of-town convention. These invitations were extended with discretion. Mr. Rand did not take his father to every Rotary luncheon nor suggest his attending the first convention held after the father came to live with the Rands, lest there be overmuch expectation on the one side and obligation on the other.

A caution here, however: nagging attempts to force an old person into socialization and participation may be as much of a mistake as allowing him to withdraw. There are some men and women, especially in advanced old age, who really want to be only spectators of others' activities or even to disengage themselves completely from everyday life and pursuits, perhaps so that they may meditate and philosophize in inner peace.

On the other hand, if your parent is the kind of person who goes out and makes friends on his own, don't discourage him no matter what you think of the company he keeps. It may embarrass and disgust you that your father loves to chew the rag with the firemen down at the firehouse, or shares a drink with every workman who comes to the house, or enjoys eating in the kitchen with the cleaning woman the day she comes. You may be outraged that your mother, who was born and bred a lady, loves to go window shopping with a gum-chewing, blond young manicurist, or delights in inviting to tea a bejeweled old harridan with a scandalous past. But you have no business disapproving or regulating or censoring your parents' friendships. Little is more annoying to children of any age than their elders' criticisms of the people with whom they choose to associate, and the right to freedom of friendship goes either way.

With your parents given every encouragement and opportunity to lead their own social life, you should also lead yours with a clear conscience. It is not necessary that you sacrifice yourself and your family to the mother or father who lives with you, and he or she ought not always to be present when you have guests, for the social life of both sides should be based on the same principles of good sense and good taste. Each of you ought to have your own friends to whom the other is friendly and who are respected; but neither should deny the difference in generations.

This does not mean, of course, that people of various ages can never be mingled successfully at a gathering, nor that just because someone is no longer young he cannot make a real contribution to a group. Often an older man or woman can be a charming and delightful addition to a gathering. The point is that if you want to live comfortably under the same roof with your parents, neither generation must take for granted complete welcome and acceptance into the friendships of the other.

Even if your parent does not fit in particularly well with your friends, you may be fortunate in having one who behaves with tact and understanding; who looks in on a party of yours, leaves pleasantly and not too obviously, and doesn't become disturbed by the noise. Or a broad hint on your part may be all that is needed to insure the privacy of your parties; something like, "Now, Mother, since these aren't your friends who are coming tonight, you needn't feel obligated to stay with us."

But many a family is tormented by an older person's persistence in being in on everything. Grandpa may not want to go to bed shortly after the company arrives. He may consider himself the life of the party and annoy and embarrass you all evening with long-winded tales and corny jokes, or, at the other extreme, may fall asleep in his chair when gaiety is at its height. Grandma may monopolize the conversation, swinging it in whatever direction she wishes, and not permitting you or your guests to get a word in edgewise to give it a turn. Or, perhaps worse, she may sit plaintive and silent in a corner, casting gloom on the festivities because she makes everyone present feel ill at ease and sorry for her.

Such situations, after some repetition, are sometimes brought to a conclusion by the desperate decision, "As long as Mother (or Father) is alive, we just can't have people here." Sometimes they engender their own unhappy endings; friends drop off, stop coming. Neither outcome, to put it mildly, is satisfactory.

If you find it difficult to veer your parent away from your parties, one measure you can take when an especially late and noisy one is scheduled is to arrange to have him stay out overnight with a friend or relative. Such an expedient, however, is scarcely feasible when you just expect a few friends for a quiet, informal evening, so for the sake of your social life and friendships as a whole you need to do some more basic, long-term grappling with the problem.

It is not an easy one to solve but here, as in almost everything involved in your care of your parents, the best thing to do is to have a reasonably frank and friendly discussion with them about the whole matter. Tell them that you expect them to act just about the same way as you do when your own teenagers have a party. You are polite, you greet the guests, you stay a bit if things work out that way, and then you leave to let the youngsters enjoy themselves. Make it clear, so your parents don't feel discriminated against or shoved out, that you'll do the same for them when they have their friends at the house. It may be that all the sweet reasonableness will be on your side, and your parent will react with indignation or hurt to the point of tears. In this case you will have to take comfort in the long view that it is better for both of you to stand on firm ground than to be on shifting sands for years—you, trying hard not to show that you wish your parents were out of the way and feeling guilty that you wish it; and they, suspecting that they are not welcome, trying to cover up how ill at ease they are.

Quite possibly, however, you may find that your parents were as confused as you about the part they should play when you entertain. They may not really want to be at your parties, likely to be as boring to them as a high school picnic to you, but are just doing what they think they ought lest you think them rude or ungracious. Your sanction of their absenting themselves may come as an enormous relief.

A clear understanding and adjustment by either or both of the adult generations in your home may be necessary also in regard to friends who are nonhuman—that is, your parents' or your pets. For some years your mother may have had a beloved and pampered cat given her by a friend when it was a tiny kitten to assuage some of the empty-house loneliness in early widowhood. But you may have a dog which does not like cats . . . so when your mother moves in with you, somebody is going to have to give, because it will not be the animals.

Or a member of your household—father, mother, one of the children—may be so allergic to dog hair that severe asthmatic attacks occur when a dog is nearby. Unhappily, Mother has a dog only slightly less dear to her than her children. Then again, the converse may be true. Granny may be allergic to dog hair, while you and your children cannot imagine home without your beagle.

It may be that the parent who moves in with you has a strong dislike of dogs (or birds or cats or hamsters or reptiles) while your family goes in for a virtual domesticated zoo. Conversely, it may be you who have this dislike and despite all the articles you have read on how good it is for youngsters to have pets, have never allowed them any. Will you similarly deny Mother her later-life joy in her French poodle?

Frankly, there is no good solution to pet problems in two-, three- or four-generational households where attachment to animals is not unanimous. The best you can do is to evaluate all the factors in the situation (or get the help of a caseworker in evaluating it) and, at a family conference, arrive at the least hurtful solution. Where allergic illness is involved, probably pets should be taboo no matter whose heart is broken. Where it is simply a question of likes and dislikes, whoever most needs the association with a pet is the one who should be given priority. This may be Grandma or Grandpa, sad in widowhood or broken by dependence, or it may be freckle-faced Johnny who, like any normal boy, benefits by loving and being responsible for Rover, or it may be retarded Ginny who desperately needs the affection and friendship she does not get from her contemporaries.

Sometimes a pet becomes the hook on which to hang grievances that go much deeper than the presence of an unwanted animal in the house. Anna McPherson who had never liked her mother-in-law and resented having to take her in, unconsciously transferred her emotions to the older lady's dog Tina. A quiet, elderly, well-behaved little mongrel, Tina spent most of the time sleeping at her mistress' feet. She had no odor, did not shed hair, never jumped on furniture, and made no mess. The elder Mrs. McPherson fed her and took her out. But to listen to Anna, Tina was an intolerable nuisance invading and pervading her life. She had to buy dog food! She had to keep vacuuming all the time! With that animal there was no peace or comfort in the house! Be aware of the possibility of such unreasonable "displacement" of emotions, whether by yourself or your parent, and you will be able to deal with this particular kind of pet situation more calmly.

Straight thinking, clear ideas, and definite shared decisions can go a long way, too, to mitigate some of the difficulties which often arise because the grandparents "pick on the children" or "spoil them."

15

THE THIRD GENERATION

WHETHER WE HAD dear old grandparents when we were young, or whether we wished we had them, most of us have set ideas about what constitutes the Perfect Grandparent. Straight out of the pages of storybooks, Grandmother is a lovely, tender old soul who adores doing for and taking care of the children when they are little and is their confidante when they are older. Likewise a product of fiction is gentle and jovial Grandfather, who makes boats and doll houses for his grandchildren when they are young, and then a few years later, charms their youthful minds with fascinating bits of information and mellow wisdom.

The chances are decidedly against your parents' fitting into this pretty picture. Whatever they were like as parents, they are likely to be as grandparents. No mystical process makes the birth of one's children's children radically alter one's personality or attitudes. If, for example, your mother was a career woman who regarded you and your brothers and sisters as rather a nuisance, she will find your sons and daughters a nuisance, too. If she abhorred reading *Winnie the Pooh* aloud to you, she won't delight in reading *The Cat in the Hat* aloud to your children. If she took pleasure in making your clothes and she is still able to sew, she will probably take pleasure in dressmaking for your children; but if she always hated needlework, becoming a grandmother won't make her like it. If your father, a scholar, irritably insisted on quiet whenever he was reading, when you were a child, the shrieks and shouts of your young hopefuls will be anything but music to his ears.

Forget idealizations, realize that grandparents don't become different from themselves because they are grandparents, and you will spare yourself untold irritation and disappointment over your parents' relationship with your children. Most older men and women find it fairly easy to be the ideal grandparents when they see their grandchildren only occasionally. But when three generations live under the same roof, the charm of the youngest for the oldest is liable to wear off very soon—often, indeed, within a few days.

Withal, association of the very old and the very young can be enriching for both. Mr. Sherman and his small grandson, of whom we told you in Chapter 2, are a case in point. So are Eugene Field's immortal old man Shuffle-Shoon and little boy Amber-Locks:*

Shuffle-Shoon and Amber-Locks
Sit together, building blocks;
Shuffle-Shoon is old and gray,
Amber-Locks a little child,
But together at their play
Age and Youth are reconciled,
And with sympathetic glee
Build their castles fair to see.

"When I grow to be a man"
(So the wee one's prattle ran),
"I shall build a castle so—
With a gateway broad and grand;
Here a pretty vine shall grow,
There a soldier guard shall stand;
And the tower shall be so high
Folks will wonder, by and by!"

Shuffle-Shoon quoth: "Yes, I know;
Thus I builded long ago!
Here a gate and there a wall,
Here a window, there a door;
Here a steeple wondrous tall

* Reprinted from *Poems of Childhood* by Eugene Field; copyright 1904 by Charles Scribner's Sons, 1932 by Eugene Field; used by permission of the publishers.

Riseth ever more and more!
But the years have levelled low
What I builded long ago!"

So they gossip at their play,
Heedless of the fleeting day;
One speaks of the Long Ago
Where his dead hopes buried lie;
One with chubby cheeks aglow
Prattleth of the By and By;
Side by side, they build their blocks—
Shuffle-Shoon and Amber-Locks.

Indeed, a grandparent can make valuable contributions to a child's happiness and emotional health. A little spoiling; joy in a child as he is, untainted with any desire to improve him; faith in his future—"He'll come out all right"—create a sense of being loved and approved which is good for any youngster, and especially good for one who is physically handicapped or mentally retarded. It is good for the older person, too, to be able to give uncritical affection. "I had a great deal of pleasure out of my own children," one grandmother said, "but never the sheer, unmitigated joy I now get from my grandchildren. With them it's all pleasure and no responsibilities."

Even if there is warmth between the first and third generations it may cool with close living or as the children grow older. Grandparents and grandchildren do not always retain a close relationship during the period between the end of early childhood and the advent of real maturity. Often adolescents think of Grandmother and Grandfather as even more stuffy and foolish and old-fashioned than those uninformed, misguided ancients, their own parents, for it takes some degree of maturity to appreciate maturity. Mark Twain expressed this by saying that when he left home at eighteen, his father was a back number who didn't know anything; but when he returned at twenty-two, he was astounded to discover how much the old man had learned in the interim.

But whatever the age of your children, you will have little Grandma or Grandpa trouble if you were blessed with the kind of parent who was always an independent kind of person and who allowed you to be reasonably independent, too.

You will have harder going if your parent is temperamentally inclined to be nagging, irritable, and interfering. Remember, however, that you cannot protect your children against Granny's aspersions on their bad manners, untidiness, loud voices, impertinence, or whatnot by trying to push her into being something she is not: someone sweet and charming with the young. "Mother, Sally would love to have you help her dress for the party," or "Father, wouldn't you enjoy going to the play at school?" and any such cooing, unrealistic, wishful attempts to get annoyance replaced by love, crankiness by benevolence, or lack of interest by enthusiasm cannot improve the situation. Deal with it realistically. Let your mother know that you know the children are a cross to her. Get her to suggest some ways and means of keeping them out of her hair. Devise some yourself. For example, if Mother pays regular long visits to other members of the family, try to have these occur during school vacations. Ask her if she doesn't think that at those trying times when youngsters are most rambunctious and all over the place, she would be better off staying in her room. Among these periods are rainy days, the rush hour on school days, the after-school invasion, and—contrary to sweet, sentimental ideas about the Children's Hour—bedtime. Doubtless you will never be able to achieve perfect harmony, but at least by utilizing rests rather than hammering away at false notes you can markedly reduce the number of discords.

Quite the opposite from the captious grandparent but likewise a family problem is the doting one who undermines all parental discipline and shamelessly spoils the children. If your parents are overindulgent with your children as a compensation for having been too hard on you, your annoyance as a parent will be intensified by your resentment as a child. If they do their pampering because they are competing for your children's affection, you will find this also hard to take. Whatever lies back of undue grandparental spoiling, however, for the sake of your family as a whole it cannot go unchecked. Ways to lessen it can range all the way from gentle cooperative discussions about what's really best for the children to a flat prohibition, "Now, Pop, if you *will* buy candy when you take Junior on late-afternoon walks, no more walks!"

Perhaps your parent maddens your teenagers with a constant barrage of questions: "Who just telephoned?" "Where are you going?" "What time did you get home last night?" "Who was at the party?" "Who's that honking for you?" This kind of prying is very likely to spring from boredom, and your mother or father with more life of their own might not feel the need to know so much about the lives of others. Encouraging your parents' interests and friendships is an excellent way to relieve your children from the strain and annoyance of grandparental curiosity. It's a good idea, too, to imply to the youngsters that though naturally Grandma or Grandpa doesn't need to know all about everything they're doing, once in a while they might volunteer a bit of information about school or social doings to give the old folks the sense that "I'm sharing my life with you." A father who tells his father something about what's going on at business sets an example for a grandson to report on a football game.

Grandpa Bassett, although a semi-invalid, was a definite asset in his son's and daughter-in-law's suburban home. George Bassett adored his three sons and daughter, but he was an executive on the way up, constantly preoccupied with business, and traveling most of the time. It was especially valuable for the boys to be able to discuss things with another man who was always accessible, which they would not have dreamed of discussing with Mother, who might not understand. Mother, who had her hands full with a household of seven, was delighted to have the boys feel close to an understanding older man.

A grandmother in the home may likewise be the only one who has time to listen to youngsters' experiences or problems. Either can uniquely provide a valuable sense of family and historical continuity and experience: "when Daddy was a little boy" or "when Grandfather (or Great-grandfather) came to the United States" or "what it was like when automobiles were new" or "before you went places on airplanes."

In some three-generation households, however, living together is grim primarily because of the younger generations' actions and attitudes towards the oldest. Mrs. Hopkins, at eighty, was dealt with by her children and, consequently, grandchildren as doddering and incompetent. Her opinions on current affairs were treated with condescension, her interests disparaged and her preferences largely ignored. There is no more reason to play down a person because he has lived many years than there is to revere him for the same reason.

After all, people are people first and belong to a certain age group only secondarily; they merit respect or disrespect for themselves, not for the number of their birthdays.

If you have a tendency to belittle a parent because he is old, it is likely to be a cover-up for the fear that you will fall back into a former childish role, and if you don't look up to Mama or Papa, why then you're safe from feeling that you ought to obey them. Bear in mind that you are not a young child and you will not have to depreciate an older person to prove it. Your children will take their attitude from yours. If they look down on your parents because of their age no grandparent-grandchildren problem will be any nearer solution. Also, you are sowing a crop which someday, to your sorrow, you will reap.

There is another way in which sons and daughters sometimes make life hard for parents who live with them, and in the long run no softer for themselves. Some couples assume that when Grandma or Grandpa joins the household they've acquired a built-in baby sitter.

Now if all grandparents were saints and martyrs, they might embrace the opportunity to devote themselves to their dear grandchildren so their dear children could go out. But since grandparents, like the rest of us, are ordinary humans, not many like the feeling that they're being used. Grandma is likely to feel put upon, unhappily resentful, if you dash out to have a good time, simply taking it for granted that she'll sit by and see that ten-year-old Willie gets to bed on time; and still more unhappily guilty that she has the resentment. While everyone else goes on a picnic, Grandpa, not requested but expected to stay home to take in the milk and feed Bobby's dog and close the windows if it should rain, will probably be filled more with suppressed anger than with a sense of loving kindness.

It makes anyone feel menial to have it taken for granted that he is always available to free others. Of course your parents will often be glad to do for you and your children, but never forget that they have the right to be asked whether and when, and they should have the privilege of being able to plan their time. Sons and daughters who inquire, "Did you have something you wanted to do?" or "Would it be convenient?" or "Do you have an engagement tomorrow night?" are likely to get more loving grandparental help and certain to create a better general atmosphere in their homes than those who blandly assume the oldest generation has no use, value, or ambition except to be at the youngers' service.

You might even offer to pay your parent for baby-sitting, as you would a professional sitter. If he refuses to accept money, as did Mrs. Lovett, you might like to copy Mrs. Lovett, Jr.'s little plan. She put "sitting" money into a piggy bank, and when it was full the whole family went on a spree on "Grandma's money."

As the good relationship between the oldest and youngest in your household will be jeopardized if you expect your parents to be at the beck and call of your children, so will it be if conversely you expect your children to give up everything for "dear Granny" or "poor Gramp, who's old." When seventy-five-year-old Mrs. Stephens came to live with her son and daughter-in-law, twelve-year-old Mary, without any question on anyone's part, was expected to give up her pretty, little-girlish room and move in with her five-year-old twin brothers. Mary felt pushed around; nobody had considered her or asked her what she had wanted to do. The little boys were indignant that their big sister had barged in on them, and made a bad situation worse with "Who wants you here?" Needless to say, the whole situation didn't endear Grandmother to the youngsters.

With a similar situation of an aging mother's moving in, and a young daughter, Rose, the Jordan family handled matters much better. In advance Rose was told that she ought generously to offer Grandma her room, although Grandma mightn't accept; also in advance Grandma was notified that Rose was going to be sweet enough to offer to give up her precious room, which had been decorated especially for her the year before, and that of course she was welcome to it, but other, perhaps slightly less comfortable arrangements could be made. True, it was a bit of a gamble, but when the little girl and the old lady were face to face each came through with a fine, gratifying sense of altruism. When Grandma said, "No, darling, you keep your own room," a heartwarming look of combined relief and affection came over the child's face.

But no matter how justly every member of your complex setup retains his or her rights; no matter how cleverly you circumvent or overcome the difficulties your parents' particular personalities may create in them as grandparents, there may still be a hazard to the success of three generations' living together. We have brought it up before, in Chapter 10: it is the tendency to fall back into the parent-child relationship of long ago. If you let yourself, you will want to be a good child and meet with Mama's or Papa's approval, and when they say "You have badly behaved children," it will seem to you as if they were still saying "You are a naughty boy (or girl)." Unless you are on guard you may be less strict or stricter with your children than you think is right; you may alter schedules, or lower or raise the standards you had set for them. As a parent, then, you will be angry at yourself for doing things to your children of which you don't and can't approve. This anger may reflect itself in annoyance with the parent whom you blame for upsetting the applecart, and altogether you may find yourself in a sorry mess.

Such confusion can be dangerously transmitted to your children. They need to know for certain which adults are in power, who represents the Supreme Court. If they are able to run to their grandparents when they don't get what they want from their parents, and vice versa, you may have to cope with behavior difficulties. Ideally every grandparent would always say, "Ask Mother or Father," when there is any question about what a youngster should do. But the temptation to usurp authority or to curry favor is so great that you cannot put all the burden of doing the right thing upon your parents. You yourself have a responsibility in asserting your parental prerogatives.

You may value your parents' advice and of course consultation with them is always in order. But in the last analysis there should be no doubt as to who has the say with your children and in order to establish and retain your position you have to be consistent. You cannot revert to asking Mom or Dad what to do as if you were a child yourself, nor can you use them for your convenience, now giving them authority and now revoking it.

All this holds true even when Grandma is in charge of the children for longer or shorter periods. Both legally and in the children's minds the parents have responsibility. They should back Grandma in acting for them whether she takes over the household because there is a new baby, or Daddy and Mommy are away on a trip, or Mother works. But unless parents' and grandparents' true roles in the family are maintained, there can be only confusion in the minds of all three generations. Mother and Father will not be Mother and Father as much as they will be the children of Grandmother and

Grandfather and merely the older sister and brother of their own children.

But the fact that it is desirable for each generation to be distinctly itself doesn't mean that the family can't be unified. After all, a cake having three separate layers is nevertheless one cake.

16

YOUR NEW FAMILY PATTERN

IN ORDER TO FEEL at ease, secure, happy, or for that matter truly alive, everyone needs a sense of belonging. And belonging, even more than charity, begins at home. An old person may feel more alone living in his children's home than all by himself in an isolated cottage or a furnished room. The whole complex, often difficult job of living together is done well only when the family—the modified family of the middle or later years which may include parents' parents and/or grandparents—is a genuine unit.

If the older members of your family in their minds or yours are going to be chronic visitors instead of an integral part of the household your family will live uneasily. For you there will be the continual strain of having to adapt yourself to your mother, father, grandmother, or grandfather with the same inevitable strain incurred by the need to adapt to any house guests, however welcome. You have probably heard the cliché about weekend visitors "You're glad when they come and glad when they go." Since elders who have come to live with you are not likely to go, for as long as they seem to be visitors there's not even an end in sight to the usual guest-in-the-house stress.

On their part, your father or mother with a guestlike attitude will expect to be treated like guests—provided with more or less entertainment, have their tastes given preference, and receive such other courtesies as go with polite hospitality. To make matters worse, being your parents, they will expect you to do the honors with a tension-creating plus—family closeness and intimacy. You are all, therefore, headed for trouble unless your parents become worked into the family setup as real family members, not left to be phony visitors.

As we have said before, it isn't easy for adults who have long been living in two separate units to combine and re-form them. Indeed, the chances are that never again will your family be as relatively simple and solid a whole as it was before, when it was "nuclear." But at least you can approach a happy and harmonious oneness. Make up your mind that there won't be any miraculous welding; it can come about only as the result of conscious, deliberate planning and realistic acceptance of the fact that you can't end friction between you by pretending that you can live quite separately under the same roof. Human beings are not like so many jars, each remaining in its own place on a shelf. They move about and they are inevitably involved with one another.

That is why the living together of Mother Watkins and her son and daughter-in-law was a failure. All three deluded themselves that they could have the same privacy as before they doubled up because the younger Watkins' apartment was sizable and Mother's room and bath could be entered direct from the front hall with no need to pass through other rooms. Also, each generation had the notion it could live its life as in separate circles touching only at one point. After twenty years of trying to act as if there were still two independent family units, the three Watkins are still getting on one another's nerves because they are constantly irritated by the obvious. As one example, of course the older lady doesn't restrict her goings and comings to passing through the hallway to her room! As another, it is not possible for the younger Watkins to keep their peculiar hours—they work on a morning newspaper and are at home all morning and out all evening—without disturbing Mother's more ordinary routines.

Often in the sunshine of filial and parental affection neither children nor parents detect potential clouds. But don't make the mistake of thinking that just because someone is your parent, and a parent you love, you can proceed to jell together in later life without effort. Sometimes thinking differently from one's parents is a form of rebellion, as against a strict religious upbringing or stuffy conventionality or conservative political beliefs. But quite without any element of rebellion it is simply and usually in the normal course of any generation's development to have ideas and ways different from the preceding one's. Take these normal differences into account when you modify your family life so you can bring your mother or father into it. Bear in mind that the successful living together of aging parents and grown children is not dissimilar from a successful marriage. There, also, individuals who have lived differently and apart must learn to create a new way of life together.

In order for your parents to become a real part of the modified family unit your living together brings about, they must, like all its other members, have some rights and privileges.

We have already discussed in Chapters 12, 13, and 14 the values for older people in having their own money, own possessions, and own friends. Furthermore, no one can really feel he belongs unless he has some actual space he can call his own. Ideally perhaps any older person ought to have his or her own bedroom, living room, and bathroom but few of us nowadays can afford such luxury for our parents. Of course if it is at all possible you won't have your mother or father sleeping in a bedroom with one of your children or on a convertible sofa in the living room.

But suppose such accommodations may be all you are able to provide. You can still give your parents the sense of having places exclusively theirs. These might include a chair definitely Grandma's or Grandpa's; a desk or dressing table, or if that's absolutely impossible, at least inviolable drawers in someone else's desk or dressing table. Be sure to provide your parents with a definite place all their own for their clothes. If no closet is available, rather than mix in their garments with yours or your children's, let decorative effects go hang in favor of emotional effects and buy a fibreboard wardrobe. Old folks so unfortunate as to have no place wholly reserved for them in their children's homes are bound to have the feeling that the family with whom they live has just moved over grudgingly to make a bit of room and is waiting with bated breath for the moment when they'll be gone.

Like every other member of the family your parents ought to have certain intangible rights and privileges, too. Because they are elderly, for example, is no reason why they should not be allowed to go in and out of the house when and as they please—providing, of course, they are considerate about such matters as letting you know when they do not expect to be home for dinner.

With the rest of the family, likewise they should have the run of the house. If they abuse the privilege, as did Mrs. Carter, cope with the situation in somewhat the same way as Mrs. Carter's daughter did. Mrs. Carter had an unfortunate way of utterly lacking respect for others' privacy; or, to put it more bluntly, she opened closed doors without knocking and snooped into bureau and desk drawers. The daughter had the place fitted with an assortment of locks, and when her mother inquired aggrievedly "Why do you lock things up?" countered with a round-eyed, amiable, yet devastating, "Why, how did you find out I did?" Granted, you won't find it pleasant to take such precautions if you've long been used to leaving things lying about freely and feeling safe from intrusion behind closed doors. But precautions and preventives are lesser evils than the annoyance and anger bound to ensue if your privacy is invaded, or if you make (probably futile) attempts to confine your parents as if they were naughty little children.

Everyone in a family acquires a sense of belonging by having certain responsibilities. Without exploiting your parents see that they have some in accordance with their strength, abilities, and tastes, always planning what they are to contribute with them and never giving assignments in the manner of a boss.

Perhaps your mother, like Mrs. Thomas, Sr., enjoys sewing; then, like that lady, she might do the family mending. In the Thomas home the children assume "Grandma fix" when anything tears as automatically as they assume "Daddy fix" when a toy is broken. Or, Mom may be one of those Victorian or Edwardian products who considers it sinful not to be up and dressed and bustling by 6:30 A.M. How about her preparing breakfast, especially if that particular chore has always marked the all-time low in the day's work for the lady of the house? It may be that her forte is flower arrangements, or that she has exceptional skill in the preparation of angel-food cake or fried chicken. If so, she might take on these arts as her special contribution to family living. An extra dividend will be the respect and approval she gets from guests.

Frankly, you'll find it a little harder to think up responsibilities to delegate to your father, especially if you live in an apartment or housing development where there is no opportunity for him to do such chores as cutting the grass or painting. But with the exercise of some ingenuity you will also be able to find things for him to do, not only useful in themselves but also useful in helping him to belong. Among them might be preparing breakfast, making minor repairs, changing light bulbs, keeping household accounts, and overseeing plumbers, painters, electricians, handymen, and similar workers who always seem to perform better for other males than for females.

In your attempts to weave your parents securely into your new family pattern it is not of course necessary or even desirable that you be together all the time. Take, for instance, the matter of vacations. Whether or not your mother or father ought to go along on them depends on a number of factors. Among these are whether they and you enjoy the same things; whether you all want to be together, or whether you need a rest from one another. The situation may not differ essentially from the one which often arises when older teenage children have their own vacation ideas and they and their parents may or may not want to vacation as a family. If you go on a long cross-country trip by automobile, for example, Grandma mightn't relish regularly spending eight to ten hours cramped in a car or sharing your chances in more or less comfortable motels. Grandpa, it is quite conceivable, might not take with the same enthusiasm as you and the children to roughing it in a mountain camp with an ice-cold lake as the only bathtub.

There is nothing wrong in itself about you and your family going on your preferred kind of vacation merely because your parent can't or doesn't want to share it with you. The Parkers sacrificed themselves unnecessarily to Mr. Parker's eighty-six-year-old father. Pop Parker spent six months in Florida, six with his son and daughter-in-law in Delaware. "And we never go away in summer," the Parkers would say self-pityingly, "because by the time Pop gets here from Florida, he has had enough of traveling." It did not occur to them that without hurting Pop at all there were several outs for them. They might have shifted the dates of his arrival and departure to allow for their taking a very early or very late summer trip. They might, since he was independent enough to be on his own in Florida, have left him at their house with a temporary paid housekeeper. They might have invited another relative to stay with him during their absence. In the last analysis, there really wasn't any insuperable practical obstacle to the Parkers' taking a vacation away from home during the summer months. What kept them tied was nothing but themselves. They made the mistake of treating the old man not as part of the family but as a guest whom it would be rude to leave.

"This is where we came in" in this chapter: we cautioned you about treating your parent like a chronic visitor. We need to warn you now about the other extreme of well-intentioned attempts to do a good job with aging parents: it is to work too hard to make your mother or father feel they belong. If you do, if your efforts to integrate them into your family group are obvious, you'll defeat the purpose of these efforts. The surest way to be unconvincing is to overemphasize, so you give yourself away and indicate that you feel your parents don't belong if you put into words or force their absorption. Accept your parents' presence in your home as long-term; be sure that they have their due rights and responsibilities in the family. Then casually let nature take its course, and you should come very near, if not all the way, to creating a family unit without disturbingly detached parts.

PART IV

Life Must Go On

17

RETIREMENT—THEIRS, OR PERHAPS YOURS

ALTHOUGH ALL ALONG we have been urging you not to rush, push, or abet your parents into premature dependence, here we want to emphasize this particularly because certain events tend to precipitate children into thinking, "Now we have to plan for them." One of these is retirement, which seems to spell out, "You are old."

Actually aging is a quite relative matter. After all, every one of us is aging from the moment he is born. Some authorities like to use "aging" for the "young-old" between sixty-five and seventy-five and "aged" for the seventy-five-year-olds through centenarians plus. But even so there is no fixed time when mentally or physically the line between maturity and old age is crossed.

A man who is still functioning at his desk or machine the last day he is sixty-four is not suddenly aged and decrepit on his sixty-fifth birthday just because he no longer has to go to work. Your parent may be younger at sixty-five than someone else's at fifty. Or, he may have young eyes and an old heart or an old back and young ears or any other combination of physiological characteristics. While there are certain fairly rare organic diseases which can cause senility long before sixty, it is quite possible for someone to pass the century mark without being in the least senile.

Occupationally, also, aging is relative. An unemployed man looking for a run-of-the mill job may be "too old" at forty-five or even forty, while a statesman, lawyer, or college professor may be in demand in his sixties, seventies, or even eighties.

How a person feels about himself has much to do with his growing old. Many a man has felt and acted younger in his sixties than he did on his fiftieth birthday. Then, despite a party and congratulations, he may have looked upon it as a kind of marker of a place from which he could only go downhill. Many a woman is mentally and emotionally more youthful in her forties when the children are reared and she embarks upon a brand-new career or reactivates an old one, than she was when she reached thirty and gloomily wrote herself off as a member of "the younger set." A change of pace or type of work may simultaneously give someone a new look at himself. For many years, hard-working newspaperman Robert Malcolm, sixty-six, had specialized in aviation. The newspaper on which he worked had no compulsory retirement policy, but Mr. Malcolm began feeling very old indeed when younger colleagues were quicker at getting scoops or aviation reporters from competing newspapers came out daisy-fresh from long, uncomfortable travel which nearly knocked him out. He decided that he was "too old" for legwork, but not too old to capitalize on his vast accumulated knowledge of aviation, resigned from the newspaper, and proceeded to free-lance. Today, in his middle seventies, writing aviation pamphlets and magazine articles more or less at his own volition and his own time, and ghost-writing speeches for airline executives, he looks and feels younger than he did in his middle sixties.

Some elderly individuals "deny" aging which can be very distressing to those who love them, for they may jeopardize life and limb. But it is better to let your parent deny that he is old than to influence him into thinking that he is older than he feels or, indeed, is. An insidious way to do this is to plead, "Now, Pop, you've worked hard all your life, and you have enough to live on" or, "We'll help you have enough to live on so why don't you retire and take it easy?" As a deterrent to well-meaning efforts to "be good to" your parent, keep in mind the fact that the period after retirement is likely not to be a brief postlude to active participation in industrial, agricultural, or professional life, but may stretch out for thirty-five more years.

The relativity of how old is old also depends upon from where one sits chronologically; an English judge once unofficially defined an old man as someone "ten years older than yourself." To a teenager anyone in the forties may be ancient; to an octogenarian, youthful. Mrs. Herter, fifty-one, a counselor in the personnel department of a large corporation, was consulted by two women employees in their early thirties about the "problems" they had with their dependent, aging mothers.

"You girls look awfully young to have elderly mothers," she said sympathetically. "How old are they?" Her own hair only about one-quarter gray, still wearing a size 10 and at the height of her earning capacity, it never occurred to her that at her age she might be considered the equivalent of an aging parent about whom anyone needed to be concerned, and she envisioned the young women's mothers as fragile, doddering, dependent old ladies somewhere beteen the seventies and nineties. To her partly amused and partly appalled astonishment, she learned that the mothers were respectively fifty-three and fifty-five, healthy and financially independent.

For statistical convenience, sixty-five is the age separating the older portion of the population from the rest. Also usually the age for compulsory retirement, it derives from the first social security plan in Germany in 1879, a time when sanitation and medical care were not as good as now, life expectancy was less, and people aged so much faster that probably today's seventy-five-year-olds compare favorably with late nineteenth-century sixty-five-year-olds.

But whatever one's perspective, or the chronological fact, retirement nearly always comes as a shock, nonetheless real although expected. Even if someone is delighted to be through with work which was monotonous or wearing or carried with it crushing responsibilities, he is likely to miss certain corollary values of regularly going to the office or plant. One is the companionship of those he sees as a matter of course, without effort. Another is the identity which comes with doing such-and-such a kind of work or being associated with such-and-such a company or agency instead of just another footloose old fellow. In these fast-moving times especially, the feeling of "being left behind" or "out of things" or "not being able to keep up" is accelerated by retirement.

Your father (or your mother, if she is employed) may react to it in any one of a number of ways, some of which you may find annoying, some admirable, some foolish. Just remember that your retiree parent is an adult whom you cannot guide as if he were a child. If you disapprove of his attempts to adjust to a new way of life, endure them. Support those you consider desirable. But above all, give him understanding. At least for a while after retirement, whether he acts apathetic and depressed or boisterously joyful, he is probably going through a critical time—which perhaps as some individuals deny aging itself, he is more than likely to deny! When a study was made of a group of healthy men about ten years after retirement, nearly all reported no difficulty in adapting to life without working. Their children, however, reported otherwise. According to them for several years their fathers had had a much harder time making the adjustment than these elderly men recalled.

Often, shortly preceding and following compulsory retirement, anger is a predominant emotion. "Here I've been working for them all these years," your father's thoughts may run. "Look at all I've done for them. Look what I've developed and built up here. My work is as good as ever, if not better. And what thanks do I get? They throw me out to put some young squirt in my place!" The imminent retiree does not, of course, articulate his anger in so many words; he takes it out by acting disagreeable, impatient, and irritable with others.

Perhaps your father, whether a business executive or a worker on an assembly line, never really liked what he was doing. In that case he may look forward to retirement as a glorious release from boredom, servitude, and the alarm clock. For a while after it he may behave like a child let out of school; traveling restlessly if he has the means, playing aimlessly, and shoving aside all suggestions as to purposeful, constructive occupation with "But it's so wonderful to be doing nothing!"

This is likely to be hard on your mother and you may be disturbed by unprecedented friction between your parents. *She* hasn't retired: she still has the housework to do, and this has become much more difficult with Dad lolling in bed long after the time when she always had the beds made, dropping ashes on the floor all the time instead of just evenings and weekends, and objecting to the sound of the vacuum cleaner because it drowns out the sound of his TV program. If your parent seems to be happy leading the equivalent of a beachcomber's life, leave him alone and don't act critical. About all you can do is stand by and let time take a hopefully healthful course. Your parents, for instance, will probably each find ways to be out of the house a few hours a day so that they are not constantly under each other's feet. Your father is likely to discover even fishing or lying in the sun or going on one luxury cruise after another or shuffleboard tournaments or hour upon hour of TV pall when the novelty of being able to indulge in them diminishes, and he may begin to cast about for more purposeful and satisfying ways of using his leisure. In Chapter 20, we suggest some ways you can help him to find these once he is receptive.

A few retirees, who for many years have suppressed their boredom with their work, cut loose and have a "last fling" analogous to the much more publicized "last fling" of the middle-aged. Not a young blonde, however, but a new way of life is likely to be involved: not a forsaking of the mate of many years so much as an unprecedented disregard of her interests and desires. Mr. Hammersley, for instance, once the corporation he had served as vice-president retired him, proceeded to buy an expensive house in California, the last place his Bostonian wife—whom he had not consulted beforehand—wanted to go. Horace Baker, a bookkeeper, after forty years of being a Caspar Milquetoast for the firm, the moment he had his modest pension, invested (and lost) all his savings in a speculative venture in one of the Caribbean Islands. At retirement age, long-time successful free-lancers may frenetically seize a regular salary or, individuals long doing well on a regular salary may, equally frenetically, eschew attempting to get another regular job and try to convince themselves that there are adventure and freedom in free-lancing. If in your opinion your father has suddenly gone haywire at retirement, again, however right you may be about his ill-considered antics, there is not much you can do except tactfully offer advice which may or may not be heeded.

If your parent really loved his work, far from rejoicing in retirement he may unhappily regard the termination of his particular job as frustration and deprivation. He may act morose and despondent for some time before and after the event. Since for years he was already doing what he most wanted to, he does not welcome the opportunity to do something else and retirement seems to shut, rather than open, a door.

Although this kind of "retirement shock" occurs among businessmen and mechanics as well as among professional men, probably it is most common among the latter, especially if they have been enjoying not only their chosen field but also their particular position and associates. Fortunately, however, if a professional person has made any kind of mark in his specialty, somebody, somewhere, under some conditions, is likely to want the skill, experience, devotion, and enthusiasm that have gone into his preretirement lifetime. A former professor of education at a large university travels about the country acting as consultant to small colleges. The faculty of a California law school is composed entirely of professors retired from other law schools. A physician who had headed a foundation dispensing millions became the dean of a medical school. A nationally known psychiatrist retired from the government became the superintendent of a county mental hospital. A retired social worker well known for her work with children was in great demand to make surveys of children's institutions. If your parent is a specialist in his field, it may take a while for him to adjust to retirement, but he is likely to come through well.

In fact, most retirees, provided they have enough to live on and reasonably good health, settle down pleasantly enough into their new life of leisure. At one time "retirement shock" was held responsible for many untimely deaths. But recent analyses of statistics indicate that retirement does not really affect longevity in one way or the other. The reason that retirement seems to be a killer is because over 40 per cent of all retirees quit work because of poor health and are therefore already liabilities. Moreover, there is not always a sharp line of demarcation between "I'm still employed" and "I'm retired and unemployed." At all occupational levels some retirees, although having been given the final paycheck or the gold watch or the farewell party, nevertheless retire gradually. They take on new work or new jobs, and quit, until they stop working altogether. The average age at which social security benefits are claimed is not sixty-five, but sixty-eight.

So far we have been talking about your parents' retirement, but everything we have said applies with equal force to your own. Indeed, it may be you who are the retiree right now, with the problems of a parent anywhere from the later seventies on up greatly complicating yours. Probably at no stage of life is it more disturbing and difficult to take on the new job of responsibility for your parents than when, elderly yourself, you are hoping to be freer of obligations than ever before. Just when retirement is cutting down your income, you may be caught in a squeeze between the financial needs of your parents and of your grown children (who may not have been as successful as you had hoped) or even of your grandchildren. Your mother or father may be afflicted with one of the mental or physical diseases to which the aged are especially vulnerable at the same time your own health is beginning to fail. The chances of your parents' ability to maintain independence, even with all possible help and encouragement to do so from you, lessen with advanced age. Although most men and women who lose a spouse remain by themselves from sixty-five to seventy-four, then they move in with others; as another example, the average age of nursing-home patients is eighty.

Nevertheless, everything we have said holds good whether you are in your forties or sixties, your parents in their sixties or nineties. Although you may be retired, you have a job that needs to be done, and to do it best you will let your aged parent remain independent insofar as possible and for as long as possible.

The Burtons, aged sixty-seven and sixty-four, respectively, are dealing beautifully for all concerned with the relatively though not wholly desirable situation they have with Peter Burton's eighty-eight-year-old mother. She still wants to live all alone in a fifty-year-old high-ceilinged, steep-staired house which she and her late husband built in what was then "the country" but is now a center of suburbia; the younger Burtons are about three miles away, in a smallish apartment. Hardly a day goes by but that Mother Burton is urged by a realtor to sell her considerable wooded acreage at a price fabulous compared to its original cost, but she loves the place and doesn't want to sell, despite a very limited income which just about covers taxes, maintenance, and her food. It is also because she loves the place that she does not accept her son's and daughter-in-law's invitation to move in with them and because they don't love it, considering it too old-fashioned and hard to maintain, that they would not want to move in with her even if asked. However, their wish is academic. They have not been asked.

Saturdays "the young people" give a hand with cleaning, washing, and enough clearing up of the grounds to prevent too much of a mess. When she was eighty-two, Mrs. Burton was operated on for cancer of the breast. "They tell me that since cancer goes slowly at my age, I won't be bothered again for five years," she said cheerfully. "Well, how much more can I expect?" During her convalescence, her son called for her every evening and took her to his apartment for dinner. But she soon tired of "eating out every night" and went back to preparing her own meals. Sundays the younger Burtons usually take her to church, and the few leftovers of errands and marketing that friendly, affectionate neighbors don't cover, they stand ready to do. The greatest respect and affection exist between the old lady and her son and daughter-in-law, and no one's retirement enjoyment is wrecked.

In a different setting old Mr. Heymann and his retirement-age daughters managed well, too. Daughter Edna, a widow, had a suburban house; Mr. Heymann liked to go out there for a weekend or Sunday and see her and his grandchildren, but he hated the suburbs as a place to live. Daughter Belle, who lived in a city apartment, was an unmarried retired schoolteacher. He enjoyed having dinner with her but when they were together long they quarreled. So Mr. Heymann rented a bedroom, living room, kitchenette, and bath in an apartment hotel, and announced his determination to live and die in his own home.

When he was eighty-two he began to have a series of heart attacks and the daughters were worried about his living alone even with help close at hand. Without much difficulty they persuaded him to engage a fifty-year-old foreign-born woman of his own cultural background, a refugee from dictatorship, to stay with him. As she slept on a day bed in the living room she did not have too much privacy but her duties were light—preparing breakfast or a snack in the kitchenette, keeping an eye on the old gentleman's state of health—and she was glad to exchange a small salary for the pleasure of living in the congenial atmosphere of the hotel. Everyone except the gossiping "friends" who said, "The poor old man, you'd think with two unattached daughters he wouldn't have to live by himself," was still pleased with the arrangement when Mr. Heymann died at ninety-one in the ambulance promptly summoned by the vigilant attendant.

Reaching retirement age, to be sure, marks a definite turning point in your or your parent's life, but often the turn can be kept tolerable at the least. Another sharp turning point in aging is bereavement.

18

BEREAVEMENT

UNLESS YOUR PARENTS are killed simultaneously in an accident you will lose one of them before the other and perhaps the first time you have to take responsibility for your father or mother will be in the midst of your own grief. The intense emotions aroused by your loss of a mother or father may make it very difficult for you to see your surviving parent's feelings any way but in the light of your own, so in your sorrow you need to be careful not to assume that what might comfort you might also comfort him or her. Don't think in terms of plans you would like to make or have made for yourself, but of what would be right for the particular kind of individual your parent is, best for a bereaved wife or husband.

After years of living and thinking and working together, an aged man and wife can have developed a closeness almost beyond the ken of the very young. The frequency with which the death of one member of an old couple is followed by that of the other within a few hours or days or weeks is more than coincidence. It is as if the two had literally become one flesh, with the death of one not only depriving the other of reason for living, but also, as if they had been Siamese twins, of the physiological stuff of life itself.

The reaction of a survivor who continues to survive when a long-standing marriage is broken by death is understandably great. But its evidences differ. The way your parent acts in bereavement is a product of individual temperament and the conventions of a locality and social group. There are wide variations, for example, in the length of the mourning period, wearing of mourning clothes, and frequency of visits to the cemetery. Your parents' beliefs in such matters may not accord with yours, but you will of course respect them and not interfere with preferred observance or nonobservance of any forms.

Only if your parent's preoccupation with rituals for the deceased is unduly prolonged or intense; if a tendency to self-immolation, to complete withdrawal from life seems to be developing need you be concerned with the way of manifesting grief. Even in such a case you cannot improve the situation either by conformance on the theory that it will make Mother or Father feel better or by attacks like "You ought to pull yourself out of it" or "You simply can't go on like this." Either course will tend to make your parent hug sorrow even tighter. The only wholesome alleviation or remedy is to encourage renewal of former interests and activities and provide opportunities for enough new ones to make him or her want to go on living with the living.

You may not be able to do this without professional help. The Family Service Association of America has an excellent film strip, with an accompanying narration on tape, *The Touch of Time,* which shows how an emotional crisis caused by death was worked out with the help of a family caseworker, in the Green family. Together Mr. and Mrs. Green had run a little store. When he died, she lost not only a husband but also a full-time occupation as she could not possibly manage the store alone and had to sell it. Losing all interest in life, she became deeply depressed, sat listless for hours, did not care about her appearance.

Both daughters were deeply concerned and both considered their mother someone to be persuaded rather than consulted, but they did not agree on what should "be done with her." One sister, rather relishing her devotion in contrast to her sister, felt that Mother should live with her. The other, a quick-actionist, was all for an old folks' home. In the film they consult a family service agency whose caseworker helps both them and their mother face the realities of the situation. Gradually, with the skilled help of the caseworker, the daughters stop arguing about the disposal of their mother, and Mrs. Green comes to the realization that the future lies largely in her own hands. By the end of the film she is working as a checker in a neighborhood grocery near the store she and her late husband owned and, once more feeling useful and occupied, has generally regained her interest in life.

Possibly, far from acting grief-stricken, your mother or father may seem to you to be actually remiss in making even a suitable appearance of sadness. Should this trouble you, you would do well to recognize that some old people look upon death more as a friend than an enemy of the one who is gone. Unselfishly giving personal loss second place, your mother or your father may be thinking, "He went before he felt that he was a burden on anyone," or "Now she won't have to suffer any more." A religious belief— "It won't be long before we meet in another and better world"—can reinforce such calm resignation. Should this be the way your parent feels about death, you cannot expect or force a show of grief you think may be "normal" or "right" or "proper."

Remember also that although, as we have said, in the last analysis reactions to death, like reactions to everything else, are individual, probably it is generally true that the younger one is, the more life that could have lain ahead, the more unfinished plans which are frustrated, the more likely one is to cry out against death. An older person tends more quietly and unprotestingly to accept what has happened.

It might happen that though your surviving parent experiences intense sorrow, it expresses itself not in tears and melancholy but in antagonism and captiousness toward you or others. Bitterness toward those who are still living when a beloved is not, although not unknown at any age, often occurs among the old. It is trying indeed for sons and daughters lovingly doing the best they know how to help Mother or Father through the shock of bereavement, to encounter nothing but fault finding and hostility instead of the appreciation or the soft, tender sadness they expect. But like all oblique outlets for human emotions, such behavior is less disturbing when understood for what it is.

Some people, having the idea that to talk about the husband or wife who has died makes a widow or widower feel sad, go to great pains to avoid arousing memories. Actually, if there is any wish on your parent's part to talk about the one who is gone, it is good to keep thoughts of him or her pleasantly alive. Talk naturally and freely about things that Father and Mother said and did and events with which they were connected—though not, of course, about their last days, how they suffered, or other depressing phases of their lives.

Shortly after a bereavement it is often an excellent idea for an elderly widow or widower to have a temporary change of interests and scene. Always, of course, without being insistent, you might do well to suggest or encourage or help arrange a trip which, according to your parent's means, might be anything from a de luxe round-the-world cruise to visiting a relative in the next county.

Then, for a while at least, allow your mother or father to continue whatever routine best brings back, without morbidness, a semblance of previous life. If a decision must be made which may drastically change this way of living, avoid hastily forcing your parent into it. Just as it takes older people more time to move physically than it does those younger, so it takes them more time to adjust psychologically. Your mother or father will not be able to work out, think through, and evaluate any proposed arrangement as quickly as you can. A plan which seems obviously right to you and other family members of your generation, an idea you have hatched and found good in a matter of days, may produce weeks or months of indecision in the aging person concerned.

If your mother or father accepts prematurely a plan under "the children's" pressure, there may be a wake of bitterness left by the feeling that "I was pushed around"; whereas the identical plan concurred in "all in my own good time" promises in the long run to work out more satisfactorily for everybody.

It is an individual matter what kind of life someone who, for many years has lived as one of two, will now lead as one. As a widow or widower, your parent may want to remain alone, or have someone move in, or live with someone else, in any of the possible ways we discussed in Part II. Or, after a while, he or she may want to establish a new home through remarriage.

19

REMARRIAGE

RAISED EYEBROWS, sneering smiles, and remarks like "There's no fool like an old fool," or "Why can't she be her age?" express the traditional conviction that there is something indecent about an aging person's interest in the opposite sex. Dating, amorous or platonic, is looked upon as a form of social life exclusively for the young; and almost always, when an elderly widower or widow contemplates remarriage, adult children are shocked, and the parent concerned expects them to object.

Nobody knows how many potentially enriching later-life romances have been nipped in the bud by such prejudices and apprehensions. But love never goes into retirement. There is no set age when sex life should be over, and therefore there is no age at which marriage is necessarily improper or in bad taste. At any time of life a marriage may be suitable or unsuitable, sensible or ridiculous, well-matched or incongruous, and at twenty, thirty, forty, fifty, sixty, seventy, or eighty, one can select a mate wisely or unwisely.

Furthermore, at any age there can be many reasons for marrying besides sexual desire. One of the strongest is congeniality. When seventy-eight-year-old Mr. Coleman married seventy-four-year-old Mrs. Brett, tongues wagged with questions such as: Was she marrying him for his money? Was he marrying her because he was tired of paying a housekeeper? What did an old boy and gal like that want to marry for anyway? The true answer was that Mr. Coleman and Mrs. Brett both loved doing the same things, and both found them more enjoyable with a companion than alone. Until the old gentleman died at ninety-two, they had a fine time together, traveling, going to concerts and art exhibitions, eating good food in good restaurants and reading good books aloud to each other. Indeed, Mr. Coleman's children enjoyed the cultivated company of their stepmother so much that after their father's death they continued to dine with her weekly as they had during his lifetime.

The desire for a home of one's own, for financial security, or for relief from sheer loneliness can also be motives for marrying or remarrying at any age. The objective of having children is, of course, primarily younger folks', although it is by no means unknown for an aging man to marry a much younger woman with the idea of founding a first or second family. The variety of human motives for marrying or remarrying are sometimes overlooked by disapproving grown children who squirm at "the indecency of it all" with specific, if unspoken, reference to sex.

But as there is more than one reason for marrying, so is there more than one for children's disliking the idea of an elderly parent's remarriage. There may be a strong feeling that it is disrespectful to the memory of the deceased parent with whom the survivor may have lived for thirty or forty years. Should your widowed or widowered parent want to marry again, bear in mind that there can be no greater proof that the previous marriage was a happy one. If anything, the desire for a second wife or husband is a tribute to the first.

Some sons and daughters have a way of wanting to make of their parents a kind of museum piece labeled "My Mother" or "My Father," and are repelled at the idea of their being lovers because they will not look upon them as people with a right to lives and interests of their own. Since throughout this book, in one way or another, we have frequently stressed the importance of granting this right to your parents, you know why such an attitude should be avoided.

There are children who, more or less frankly, dread a parent's remarriage because it may mean that money will go out of the family. As a rule, this fear is greater in the case of Father than of Mother, because often estates are left so that a woman cannot will them as she wishes. It is greatest, perhaps, when the new wife is youngish and there is the possibility of a second family. There is no answer to this kind of objection for those who put money above their parent's happiness, and those who don't won't have the objection.

If an aging parent chooses a mate of similar age, the children may be worried about having, at some time in the future, to take care of not one but two old people; or, indeed, if the worst came to the worst, to care for one old person to whom they're not even related. If you are concerned over the possibility of having additional responsibilities, don't overlook the brighter side of the picture. An aging parent's remarriage may prevent forever his having to live with one of his children.

Sometimes children's worries and frettings over a parent's remarriage are on grounds of incompetence: "He can't really know what he's doing." But if your parent is reasonably able to manage himself and his affairs in general, there is no reason to assume that he isn't also competent to manage affairs of the heart.

Even added all together, the tizzies and objections which upset sons and daughters cannot overbalance the good which can come to a lonely surviving parent through remarriage. Bear in mind that your parent is old enough to know what he is doing; grant him his right to sexuality and companionship and enjoyment and the feeling of being part of the world in which having a mate is a powerful element; don't be a wet blanket and you cannot go far wrong. If it is within your power, see that there is a pleasant wedding and reception; even if you are not enthusiastic about your stepmother or stepfather, accept him or her graciously, and you will be helping your parent to keep the individuality and independence of which, in doing your job, you want never to lose sight as a goal.

20

WORK AND PLAY

HOWEVER WELL CARED for a person may be physically, however happy in all personal relationships, rarely does he feel complete without the sense that he still plays a part in the community. Too often sons and daughters who otherwise do a fine job of caring for their parents forget that good relations at home can't be maintained unless the old folks also maintain relations with what lies outside their own four walls. If your parents are in the same place where they have always lived, continuing their contacts and activities might be all that is necessary. But if they have moved from somewhere else, you may need to take a more positive part in helping them to have outside interests. A life of isolation and inactivity for your parents is a pretty sure way of creating sick and soon helpless old people, bored and complaining individuals in both the older and younger generations, and trouble in general for those who live together.

The painting, Whistler's *Mother,* although esthetically valuable has done much psychological damage. Too many of the old and young alike seem to make the serene, sitting old woman an ideal and want all older women (and men) to be similarly serene and sitting. Often children are provoked if their aging parents do not conform to this image, and often the old fit into it because it seems to be expected long before they must or should. Few women who have led an active life can comfortably hold the pose of Whistler's *Mother,* however, from the time their children no longer need them until they die. Most normal people are happier and stay in better mental and physical health at any age if they are occupied than if they are idle.

There is, to be sure, a minority of aging men and women who really prefer being spectators of the parade of life rather than among its marchers, and enjoy themselves quietly watching what goes on around them in the world at large, their homes, or the corridors of an institution. There are also some who, although healthy in mind and body, especially in advanced old age prefer to withdraw from even observing and get profound satisfaction exclusively from contemplation, their memories, and philosophizing about the meaning of their long lives. Some authorities on the aged believe on the basis of research that there is a natural course in growing old as there is in growing up and that this sometimes manifests itself in a gradual "disengagement" from persons and pursuits related to the present. James Stanley, still brilliant and robust at eighty-one, seemed quite contented unsociably to do what to others seemed like nothing, although once he had been a dynamic, influential personage in the thick of national affairs.

"You've had such an active, exciting life," someone younger said to him. "Don't you miss it?" He shook his head. "I was always so busy," he said, "that I never had time to be all by myself and think. Now I have the time, and"—he smiled shyly and engagingly—"you know, I find that I greatly enjoy my own thoughts!"

Obviously children should not attempt to obtrude upon healthy, satisfying "disengagement" by nagging to go here or there or to do this or that. But socially or physiologically caused withdrawal is something else. Your parent may act uninterested in the world of current reality because he feels despondently that it has no place for the aged and he is useless, or he may be the victim of an organic disorder affecting his brain. (See Chapter 22.) A psychiatrist or other physician knowledgeable about the aged will be enormously helpful in determining the wholesomeness or unwholesomeness of the situation if your parent seems to be disengaged and, consequently, in determining your wisest course in relation to it. In most cases, however, it is probably better to err on the side of stimulating your parent's interests, giving him the opportunity for occupation, and helping him to be outgoing and necessary to his fellow men.

A great deal has been said and written about the inestimable value of handcrafts and hobbies for the aging. In a number of cities there are periodic hobby shows of ceramics, woodwork, sculpture, painting, needlework, weaving, and many other productions of men and women over sixty or sixty-five. A growing number of classes for older people teach various handcrafts. All this is fine as far as it goes, but actually it doesn't go very far. "Busy work" is no panacea for displacement from a real position in society. It takes more than the production of a bookend or vase to make anyone feel that he still really "belongs" in the world in general. As it is vital for your parents to feel useful in their own home or yours, so it is vital to have them feel useful in the community—and this involves some give-and-take with one's fellow men.

The same holds true of collectors' hobbies. A man who has been an ardent stamp collector all his life is likely to want to continue to collect stamps when he is retired and certainly should be allowed to do so. But it is just plain nonsense to present something like stamp collecting as a wholly satisfying substitute for having been president of a corporation, head chef in a great hotel, a busy master electrician, a truck driver, or any of the occupations with which an active, gainfully employed man has been used to filling his days.

Think what it would be like to propose to a modern woman, a Ph.D., who has been engaged in important scientific research, to substitute for such work the china painting which was an enviable accomplishment of genteel young ladies in the 1890's! Yet time and time again it has been suggested that after one passes a certain birthday, the equivalent of china painting is security against boredom and a sense of futility, a guarantee of self-fulfillment.

Handcrafts and hobbies have their place, to be sure. For men and women of any age they can be important as a means of passing time enjoyably or releasing tension or as a focus of interest or as concrete evidence of achievement. We certainly do not intend to disparage them as an avocation. We aim only to cut through the foggy thinking which glorifies them as a vocation.

We caution, also, against urging handwork or hobbies upon your parent. These cannot with any benefit be thrust upon anyone. A hobby which develops out of normal, natural interests, however, can be an excellent means to an end. For example, bird watching or checkers may lead to congenial companionship. Suggesting what your mother or father might take up, exposing them to exhibits and demonstrations, is about all you can do.

If your parent, like many older people, has intellectual curiosity and wants to learn, he might like to enroll in a course for adults. Perhaps it will be in a subject entirely new to him, like the old lady who took up algebra at eighty-one because it was something she had "always missed." Or perhaps it will be a continuation of previous interests, such as the literature of a foreign country whose language he knows, or advanced history, or politics. Or, if he is planning to travel, he will have good motivation to learn at least some smattering of a new language so that he will not feel entirely cut off from communication with the man in the street and children in Latin America or Europe. The local Board of Education or university can advise on what courses are available. Some fine research and creative writing also have been done by men and women well along in years, and your father and mother might make valuable contributions to society and gain a sense of still being very useful themselves as an outgrowth of continued education.

Even if adult education does not lead to anything so specifically productive or is on a relatively elementary level, it has its very definite uses. There is, for instance, gratification to a foreign-born old person in learning to speak correct and fluent English for the first time. But like the value of hobbies in keeping old folks feeling contented and fulfilled and as if they were still part of things in general, the value of adult education can be exaggerated. Indeed, for some aging men and women it has no value at all. If your parent doesn't have the slightest desire to "go back to school" you can no more force organized adult education upon him than you can get the proverbial led horse to drink.

There are subtle ways, however, in which you can encourage your parent to be mentally active. The TV screen is often (justifiably) maligned as a soporific, an opiate, a means of spectator sport, before which the spectator sits hour after hour in a glued, glazed fashion. But this need not be if TV watching is planned. Your parent may not have the initiative to read carefully the programs offered each day, or he may not have the vision to read small newspaper print. But if you take the little time and small trouble to circle with a red pencil and call his attention to the documentary programs which will help to acquaint him in depth with what is going on in the world, to first-rate dramas and concerts and fine old movies, you are in effect exposing him to adult education in his own home or yours. Also, you might call his attention to current magazines and new books and deliberately leave them where he will see them, before or after they have been in the limbo of the room where you habitually read in bed.

Another part of life, but not all of it, is recreation. Sometimes its role is exaggerated, as in the "How jolly to be old!" articles which drool over the unmitigated joy of having all the time you want for fun instead of having to go daily to work or serve your family. But often it is underrated, especially by children who deny it to their parents.

There may be simple ignorance of the fact that recreation is as much needed by the older age group as by any other. There may be the feeling that it's not "dignified" for Mama, at seventy, to go square dancing in a public hall. But probably most usual is the loving but deadening objection, "It's too much for you."

This attitude is evident between the lines of a newspaper description of a woman's one hundredth birthday party. Children, grandchildren, great-grandchildren, and great-great-grandchildren, some of them traveling all the way across the continent, assembled for the celebration, which like many other parties, included dancing. "All this is joy for me," said the old lady, "and I want to take part in it." "And only the strongest dissuasion," reads the item, "kept her from joining in the dancing." One can almost hear the cruel kindness of the devoted descendants: "Now, now, Grandma!" or "The very idea!" or "You just sit and watch, dear," or "Don't you dare," or "You'll get sick."

Let your parent enjoy recreation of his choice; help him to find where it may be had. Most large cities have a board of recreation or a recreation council. If you cannot get the information you need locally, write, or better still suggest that your parent write, to the State Council on Aging which exists in about two-thirds of the states, or the National Council on Aging, 49 West 45 Street, New York, New York 10036, to learn what facilities for older people's recreation exist in your community.

Under public, philanthropic, or religious auspices there are golden age clubs, senior centers, and similar associations. The best of these are more than places for craft and entertainment. Their aim is to provide organization for lives no longer centered around a daily occupation. They become virtually little communities self-governed by their members who, to qualify, usually have passed their sixtieth or sixty-fifth birthdays. Your elderly parent might enjoy being a member of a band, or a folk dancing or drama group, or a baseball or bowling team in which he gets no more winded and moves no more slowly than the rest. He might want to play checkers, chess, bingo, croquet, shuffleboard, and other games with contemporaries. A few recreational groups for the elderly have successfully experimented with camping.

No prejudice against "public welfare" or "taking charity" should stand in the way of your parent's using any free recreational facility, for he is as much entitled to it as your child is to sharing in story hour at the public library or using a public playground. But if he does not choose to fraternize "with a bunch of old folks like me," that is up to him. Perhaps between the two of you you will be able to find a mixed-ages place for recreation where grayheads do not feel unwelcome.

If there is no organized provision for adult recreation in your community, you and your parents would do well to stir up interest in its establishment; old people are citizens, too, who have a citizen's rights, privileges and responsibilities. But meanwhile, your parent need not be entirely deprived of recreation with contemporaries. Let him gravitate on his own to wherever the informal gathering place of the older people in town may be, as the drugstore, perhaps, is the informal club room for teenagers. This might be the proverbial cracker barrel, or the firehouse, or even—as in one town—the poolroom, not usually a hangout for respectable grayheads. In one large city, a group of well-to-do retired businessmen, none of whom had ever laid eyes on one another before they had reached their eighties, foregather regularly near a park entrance at a certain spot which they affectionately dub "The Riviera."

Volunteer service, once almost exclusively the domain of well-to-do young matrons, now provides a growing opportunity for both elderly men and women to continue to feel useful, particularly those who cannot afford financial help but can give generously of their time. At one extreme your mother may say dismally, "What a foolish idea–who would want *me?* I'm too old," and at the other want to barge ahead on her own visiting the sick or carrying food to the poor in the individualistically benevolent fashion of the lady bountifuls of her childhood. Disabuse your parents of both ideas by explaining that nowadays effective volunteer service is organized and professionally directed, and that some agencies not only welcome elderly volunteers but have special programs for selecting and assigning them on the basis of their personality, skills, and preferences.

The Veterans Administration, for example, publishes a pamphlet "Senior Citizens—We Need You!" which asks retired, older citizens to share their experiences, friendship, and hobbies with veteran patients. At one VA hospital about one-fifth of all volunteers are over sixty; they are taught to conduct bingo games, show movies, and to help in occupational therapy and clerical and library work. At another, an eighty-six-year-old woman volunteer, who serves twice a week, visits and feeds helpless neurological patients, spends time with the tuberculous, assists with a special weekly Protestant service, and teaches Braille to two blind patients! The Peace Corps has some openings for elderly as well as youthful volunteers; the ages of a few run up to seventy-five. A number of branches of the Jewish Women's Council have "Helpmate" projects doubly beneficial—to those who are "tired of being retired" and to those whom they serve as volunteers in a wide variety of ways. Older men and women giving only as many hours or days each week as they please, work in hospitals and charitable institutions at anything from office work to carpentry, from taking patients to the bathroom to acting as receptionists for visitors. Many Red Cross "Gray Ladies" are also gray-haired. "Friendly Visitors" sponsored by public welfare agencies and churches, perhaps under another name, likewise are usually wide open to elderly volunteers who visit the homebound or institutionalized aged who are lonely and friendless, do errands for them, remember their birthdays, help with their grooming, and altogether give the kind of services one expects from personal friends.

Although some old people welcome younger visitors, there are others for whom nobody does as much good as a contemporary. For instance, the calls made by an eighty-four-year-old Friendly Visitor upon eighty-two-year-old Mrs. McGinnis, confined by heart trouble to a third-floor room, did as much good as the doctor's. The two old ladies would discourse at length upon their respective aches and pains and ailments, but Mrs. McGinnis would say later, "My, how it does cheer me up and give me hope for meself to think that her, older than me, and with all that the matter with her, is able to come up them stairs like that!"

Day-care centers for the children of working mothers have successfully experimented with having "grandmothers" assist the trained teachers by performing such services as passing milk and fruit juice and helping the children on and off with their wraps. Working with children in day-care centers for the retarded, they have a special value because of their tendency to be slower-moving and more patient than many younger volunteers.

Contrary to the usual notion, male patients, particularly in mental hospitals, are sometimes happier to be visited by white-haired, maternal women than by glamour girls. A growing number of volunteers give service of various kinds to mental patients, many of them so forlorn and friendless and so long in a state hospital that someone from the outside world who shows interest in them comes as the breath of life. The local mental health association can tell you about opportunities for volunteers in mental hospitals for those on in years. The local council of social agencies or department of welfare are sources of information for others.

Helping to find a spot for your parents as volunteers, however, is only a beginning of what you can do to maintain their sense of personal usefulness and belonging in the community. Keep up a continuing interest in their activities, for the more important they feel what they are doing, the more it will give them a feeling of prestige and the greater will be their contentment. Get them to talk about their experiences. Respect their appointments and responsibilities in connection with their service, and if you provide their transportation, help them to arrive promptly and regularly, for it is essential that their volunteering be regarded as seriously as if it were paid work. Of course, though, you cannot go to extremes of putting their commitments always over and above yours or anyone else's in the family; here, as in all successful working things out together, each one has to yield something somewhere sometime, and after all, there are taxis and friends and neighbors to call upon in case Dad or Mom can't be chauffeured by you to the place where they work as volunteers.

Now it is quite possible that if your parent has always been a wage earner, volunteering won't meet his or her need to belong. People who have known what it is to earn money tend to feel that the ability still to earn is a mark of not being old; that as long as you can get paid, you are not quite on the shelf. If your parent needs this reassurance of payment for work in this world, don't try to dissuade him with a well-meant "Now, Dad, we're only too happy to take care of you," or "Why, the idea of your thinking you must still make money at your age!" or "Whatever will people think of us if you work for pay?" The tendency to discourage mothers from gainful occupation is probably stronger than the tendency to discourage fathers, as many younger women, too, are discouraged from taking paid employment on diverse, more or less rational, grounds. Earning even a little money might make all the big difference between your parent's being able to live alone or having to live with you. But although to some extent your parents remain dependent, it is wrong—when they want to earn at least some money of their own—to deprive them of the chance to do it. Also, it may be important to a person who can still have gainful employment, especially during the latter fifties or early sixties to earn money during enough quarters to qualify for social security benefits. It may be that an elderly person needs only one or a few additional quarters to qualify. You and your parent can get all the data and instructions from your local social security office. (See Chapter 12.)

Much ink and much breath have been used in proclaiming the difficulties of older people in keeping and getting employment. Indeed, so familiar and oft-told is the tale of compulsory retirement at sixty or sixty-five, and turndowns of job applicants with gray hair, that there is no point in our even repeating it here.

We could go on and on about the shortsightedness and injustice of such policies. We could point out the senselessness of arbitrary age limits for employment when some people are healthier and younger at sixty than others are at thirty. We could call attention to the skills wasted by compulsory retirement. We could dwell on the terrifying prospect of economic imbalance in the fact that the aged, a growing proportion of our population, are being impoverished, and the diminishing proportion of younger folks are going to have to support them. We could castigate employers for their present policies and indicate ways in which various kinds of positions could be adapted to make them feasible for the elderly. We could cite instances of older men and women who make excellent workers.

But we are not writing a book for employers. Nor is this a sociological treatise, nor a plea for what ought to be. It is a book for grown children faced with how to do best by their aging mothers or fathers, and it is restricted to what exists here and now. So when we have said what everyone knows, that for older people employment opportunities in industry are limited, that retirees may be exploited and that many post-retirement-run small businesses go on the rocks, we can proceed from there.

Some senior centers make it possible for what is made there to be sold with the proceeds going to the producer. Some offices of state employment services make special efforts to place older workers. There are Community-Chest-supported agencies which likewise give them special vocational counseling and try to find employment for them; the local council of social agencies will know whether any such service exists where your parent lives. But the resource of organized, skilled vocational assistance is not the only one. Individual ingenuity is another.

In helping your parent to do something for pay, you would both do best to forget regular jobs secured through the regular channels. Suggest that he think outside of these, in terms of work rather than of employment. A former hobby, for example, might be the means to earnings now. All the years he had worked as an office manager, Mr. Lyle used to enjoy upholstering in his own home and for friends. When, in accordance with company policy, he was retired at sixty-five, he converted his basement into an upholstery shop. There he took in chairs and sofas to be worked on when and as he pleased.

Similarly Mr. Cogan, whose hobby had been furniture refinishing during his employment as a government scientist, found in his later years plenty of customers glad to give up quick delivery for fine and loving craftsmanship. Mr. Gutman had always gardened as a hobby. Beginning at the age of seventy, he ran a pleasant little business selling the exceptionally good iris, azaleas, and rosebushes which he had been developing. Then there was Mr. Cox, who had always loved puttering about with printing. In his old age, at reasonable rates, he took on printing orders which he filled in his woodshed at practically no overhead.

Women who have never worked outside their own homes have occasionally developed an individualized product which they sell in their later years. It may be an especially delectable plum pudding made from an old family recipe, an unusual kind of jam, a unique stuffed animal, or a novel pot holder. Move cautiously, however, in encouraging your mother to market her particular specialty, despite all the rags-to-riches magazine stories you have read about enormous businesses which started with no more than a nickel and a bright idea. First, she ought not to be led to expect to make much more than pin money. Second, neither she nor you should attempt to market her product yourselves. Cast about for some organization like a Woman's Exchange to handle it; usually nonprofit, such outlets exist for the purpose of enabling women to earn at home. Third, don't assume that because your mother's work is remarkable for her age her product will automatically be successful. An article is no more likely to catch on just because its maker is old than because she is young.

A country doctor, far too old and infirm to go out in all weathers and at all hours, as full responsibility for a practice would have demanded, acted as consultant to his young successor. He would ride about with the younger man as he made his rounds, getting out of the car only in case of a particularly puzzling situation. The young man would go to the car to report his diagnosis and recommendations, and everyone was happy. The patients, with confidence in the old doctor, welcomed his confirmation of the young doctor. The young doctor was glad to have the old man's advice. And the old doctor was still making his contribution to the community.

Living in an enlightened old people's home, which encourages rather than discourages its residents to remain independent as long as possible, is a music teacher. She cannot carry an eight-hour-a-day program, nor does she have enough money left to afford a studio, but once or twice weekly she goes to the homes of a few pupils.

Even without preparation for gainful employment, some elderly people, with ingenuity, have found just the right kind of work for themselves. There was, for instance, Count de Grandbord, son of a French nobleman and an American mother who, until he was sixty, had never had to earn a penny in his life. When at that age he had nothing but a small inheritance to enable him to live in the style to which he was accustomed, he cast about for something he could do. He found it as curator of a historical mansion; in exchange for his presence a few hours a day, he had enough supplementary income to pay for occasional meals in the best restaurants. Not only did he enjoy his guardianship of the mansion's elegant furnishings, but also his lifelong interest in history and his knowledge of antiques, combined with his charmingly courteous reception of visitors, made him uniquely ideal for the job. Somewhat similarly, gently bred Mrs. Johnson, widowed with an inadequate income, found herself a delightful position as executive secretary of a collectors' society.

Perhaps your father, with a quite different background, has been a mechanic or laborer. There are still some things he can do. In many localities with demand for a careful, skilled, old-time worker with a conscience and genuine interest in his work, he should never lack the opportunity to do odd jobs. Once in a while a specific request comes along for older employees. Some elegant apartment houses want staid, elderly doormen in preference to youngsters because they give more of an impression of respectability, solidity, and refinement. A state, with the double purpose of getting responsible collectors on a toll road and helping people who need to supplement their social security benefits, sought toll collectors sixty-five and up. The men work four to six hours a day during peak traffic periods; one, now seventy-four, was hired when he was over seventy.

If your mother has always been a hard-working housekeeper for her own family or others, she, too, should be in demand for anything from a few hours' baby-sitting to helping out for longer periods during illness or other emergencies in a family. Some elderly former housewives make excellent resident managers of apartment houses or YWCA residences and housemothers in girls' schools and colleges.

If you have a small business, such as a stationery store or filling station or delicatessen, which is cooperatively staffed by your whole family, by all means let your parent have a share in its work and earnings—though not, of course, simply as a kind of errand boy or janitress.

If your parents have been on a salary or wages all their preretirement lives, they may be excited over the possibility of starting their own small business such as a gift shop or dry-cleaning service or motel, or, in a rural setting, of growing and selling some kind of plants or breeding animals. Some such later-life ventures are very successful, but many fail. Question and caution your parents if they are considering one. What do they really know about running the kind of project under consideration? How thoroughly have they investigated the possibilities of its success in the neighborhood where they plan to start it? Are they sure that someone with an axe to grind is not exaggerating the opportunities for profit in the field? How much can they afford to lose and how long can they get along before the business or farm begins to pay? Urge them to get advance information and authoritative advice from the Small Business Administration, U.S. Department of Commerce, Washington, D.C. 20416, or from the Bureau of Plant Industry or Bureau of Animal Industry, U.S. Department of Agriculture (which might refer them to their county agent) Washington, D.C. 20250.

These are just a few suggestions as to the kinds of work an older person might do which we hope will lead your parents to think of many others. Remember that although they will have to venture off the beaten track to a company's employment office, you should not expect your mother or father to become another Grandma Moses. The possibility of hitherto unsuspected genius suddenly flowering at an advanced age is an intriguing one, but you would be no wiser to base your thinking and planning upon it than you would be to direct your son's education on the probability that he was going to be President of the United States. Much of the propaganda about the possibilities for a happy and productive old age has overemphasized exceptional achievements. You would do well to remember that if your parents have not made their mark by this time they're not likely to now, and to center your occupational planning with them around what they have been and are, not what you hope they might be.

A monkey wrench might unfortunately be thrown into your parents' gainful employment by either your or their unfavorable attitude toward it, or both. Though everyone has an idea of things that are "unsuitable" for a particular aging person to do, everyone's idea of what these are seems to be different. Take, for instance, the case of Mrs. Draper. She had been brought up as a "lady" and as a lady she was an expert needle woman. Often, for the fun of it, she had made exquisite dresses for her daughter and granddaughters. Yet when her fortune went with the wind and her daughter suggested that she sew for friends, she became indignant. "As if I'd be a seamstress in my old age!" she objected.

Her friend Mrs. Roberts, on the contrary, though similarly reared, seized the opportunity to capitalize on her skills. Mrs. Roberts, suddenly caught without any money, sold dainty maids' apron sets to the wealthy friends whom she had had all her life. Of the two old ladies, she led by far the fuller, more contented life.

You cannot do much about a mother who considers it beneath her dignity to be paid for something she formerly produced as an amateur. But you can avoid falling into attitudes of false pride yourself. Recognize that if the community puts a cash value on something your mother or father can do, this is desirable rather than undesirable. The fact that you are a doctor is no reason your father shouldn't be an elevator starter if he chooses. The fact that you can support your mother is no reason she oughtn't to sell part time in a department store. Don't assume that your parents can't or shouldn't work. If they want to work, not only should you let them, but you should also be ready to help them look into possibilities of how, when, and where.

A host of work opportunities for elderly people are overlooked. In a typical American community, for example, although one may hear much about lack of opportunities for its aging citizens, quite a few went begging for lack of takers. Many a working mother was screaming for someone to do the mending and minor alterations which, though not exhausting, take up hours of time. Though this would be excellent occasional work for elderly women, it was hard to find one for it. A writer repeatedly advertised for a part-time secretary; hours were practically at the secretary's preference and there was no necessity to report in bad weather, yet none except young women ever applied. Another advertisement (placed by the local newspaper to secure solicitors) read simply, without further explanation, "Excellent opportunity for retired men to supplement income by working few hours a day." It could not, therefore, have been the nature of the work which brought practically no response.

Too often an older person is indignant over the idea of doing anything he considers as having less prestige or importance than what he has done before. If your parents have this kind of attitude, maybe you can do nothing with them. But then again you may be able to help them to face today's reality. You might bring up instances of happily working old people who have adapted their former work to present circumstances. The old doctor now acting as a consultant, whom we mentioned before, is one of them. So is the former professor of literature who, retired by a university, conducts classes in current books in the houses of prosperous middle-aged ladies. A former artist has substituted occasional work in a museum for strenuous full-time jobs in advertising agencies. An actress in her seventies teaches voice and diction.

For a few hours a day, while a tailor has to be out of his shop, customers are received and the telephone answered by a seventy-five-year-old seamstress whose eyesight has become too poor for her to pursue her former trade. Able to discuss customers' sartorial problems with them intelligently, she is more valuable to the tailor than a young clerk without sewing experience, and for herself there is the life-giving interest of still being "in the business." A retired practical nurse, no longer up to working at eight-hour daily jobs, goes twice a week to a boarding home to give three mildly senile old ladies such personal services as baths, shampoos, and nail cutting. Paid for by their children, this grooming not only gives the retiree a supplement to her income from social security, but also enables the old ladies to fit in with the others in the boarding home and remain there. Even a bizarre specialty can be adapted after regular employment is over. There is, for instance, an expert on snails, especially on a species which carries a tropical disease, who, after mandatory retirement from the staff of a foundation, is a part-time consultant to the ministry of health in a Mediterranean country.

These are not pathetic comedowns. They are, rather, sensible successful adaptations to a certain phase of life, like the substitution of golf for tennis at another one. Anyone, whether paid or volunteer, who continues to help the wheels of the world go round, is no has-been.

PART V

As They Grow Older

21

OLD AGE EXPECTANCIES

EVERYONE KNOWS that as he grows older his parents are growing older too. Everyone knows the physical signs of aging, such as wrinkled skin and hair graying or falling out. Yet in combination these latent awarenesses can be sharply brought out into the open, and the first time you really notice "Mother (or Father) looks old!" can come as a distinct shock.

Watch out for your response to it, for you are all too likely to want to take "dear little Mother" or "poor old Dad" under your wing. You may transpose what was once "Mother knows best" into "I know best for Mother" and indulge affectionately in mother smothering. Warming the air with good intentions, you may try to make Father henceforth give a sorry hothouse imitation of the lilies of the field. Not only may your realization that they've grown old lead you to force your parents into dependence long before enfeeblement makes it necessary, but also, by overdosing them with care, loving kindness, fussy attention to their minor discomforts, and sentimentality—for all the world as if you were nursing a seriously ill bed patient—you are likely to accentuate any disabilities they may have.

The physiological processes which take place in later life are as normal a part of life as those which occur at puberty. Old age is no more a sickness than is adolescence.

Indeed, a growing body of evidence indicates that a number of conditions formerly believed to be an intrinsic part of getting old, among them hardening of the arteries and higher blood pressure, are not caused by time but by disease.

True, with aging come some declines such as failing senses and muscular flabbiness. But these gradual changes do not occur at the same time of life and in the same way for everyone. It is, therefore, a mistake in helping your parent to plan to have set concepts of what applies to someone sixty-seven or seventy-four or eighty-three. Think, rather, of your father and mother as individuals who have had certain experiences, abilities, and interests and base your responsibilities toward them on a combination of their personality—which is a lifelong product—their present physical limitations, and their emotional reactions to these limitations.

The family of sixty-eight-year-old Mrs. Wickersham, after some trial and error, finally managed to cope with the problem which arose when Mother became quite hard of hearing. Although she had always been so charming, gracious, and interesting a woman that she was welcome in any group, she became socially impossible because she refused to admit that she could not hear what was going on around her. The harder everyone tried to make her understand the conversation, the more she would complain that she was being "left out" or "being talked about." "Mother, if you would only get a hearing aid!" the children pleaded, but Mother, with unprecedented irritability and infuriating stubbornness, continued to counter, "I don't need one! I can hear perfectly well!" Ultimately, an old friend, who herself had had to take to a hearing aid, induced Mrs. Wickersham to try one. Now the children wisely and understandingly sustained their mother through the difficult period of adjustment to it. By experimenting with the hearing aid themselves, they developed some feeling about such discomforts as hearing noises which are too loud and too sudden; and they let their mother know that they sympathized with her tribulations and her reluctance to use the device.

Mrs. Wickersham, like many another aging person, was rebelling against the sensory evidence of age, and, in essence, was proclaiming, "I won't be deaf! I won't!" Another common response is to go to the opposite extreme and give in supinely, "What's the use of trying? I'm done for anyway." Because of weakening eyes, for example, nowadays your mother or father may merely sit instead of doing the handwork or reading that was once a source of pleasure and, if you propose going to the oculist's, they may tell you, "I wouldn't bother, it really doesn't matter." No flat "You ought to" of yours will get your parent, if he has this attitude, to take to eyeglasses, but what you might do is subtly re-interest him in enjoyment through the use of his eyes. Some people will use a magnifying glass in preference to eyeglasses, so try providing one with some face-saving comment like "My, the way they do print these days!" Hand him something he'd really like to read, like a letter from a well-loved relative or a journal containing a news item about a crony.

Most of us recognize the true situation when old people don't hear or see well, but often we don't realize that along with the other senses, taste and smell become weaker too. When old people complain that the food "doesn't taste good" daughters and daughters-in-law especially become distressed, taking this as a reflection on their cooking rather than as a fact of aging life. Find out what your mother or father most relishes, provide good nourishing food, and then don't worry overmuch about their lack of enjoyment of it. Mealtimes assume inordinate importance when a person does not have enough to do, as during a hospital stay. If your parent is busy, food won't be his major concern.

An aging parent's complaints, direct or indirect, about "what I can't do any more" are often irritating to children. Complicated by the desire to remind others "What I put up with!" and "You ought to accommodate yourselves more to me" these may take such forms as "Nobody helps me up the steps" or "I wish the children would put back the footstool when they move it." Although a natural enough part of the struggle against getting old, complaining can definitely be aggravated and increased by boredom. When, therefore, you help your parents to find something to do which seems to them useful, you kill two birds with one stone. Directly, it diminishes or does away with boredom. Indirectly, by proving that "useless" and "old" are not identical, it lessens the need to fight against aging.

Frequently old people voice continuous physical complaints because of an unconscious craving not to be ignored. Their hypochondria can be anything from annoying to infuriating to children who do not realize that it is essentially pathetic. If your parent constantly tells you about his aching back or constipation or headaches or heart (?) pains or any other one of thousands of possible ailments, try to find out whether his complaining will be lessened if he gets attention from you and your family, if he participates more in family projects, and, if possible, acquires some status and recognition in the neighborhood.

Nevertheless, pay attention to specific complaints until a doctor rules them out as having no organic basis, for they may have good grounds. The Wilder family, who had given Mom half a dozen carefully fitted, expensive pairs of shoes, were annoyed when, a year later, with the shoes all still in excellent condition, Mom complained that this pair hurt her here and that pair there, and altogether she was miserable in all of them. But the Wilders were wrong to put this down merely to elderly cantankerousness. As muscles become flabbier feet grow larger, and poor Mom was actually suffering from shoes which no longer fitted her. You may not like to have Dad shuffling about in bedroom slippers when you have elegant dinner company, but before you condemn him as "sloppy" or "inconsiderate" of you and your niceties, find out whether there may not be cause for his prejudice against wearing his shoes.

Almost always, old people's fussing about drafts and changes in temperature has a genuine physical basis: they are more susceptible than younger folk to both atmospheric and temperature shifts. But you can't seal yourself and your family up in a hothouse and you mustn't become worried over your parent's chills or sensitivity to dampness. Make sure that there is a pleasant warm corner in which he can sit, provide a sweater or shawl, be reasonably sympathetic with his discomfort, and then don't dwell on it. Above all—as we cannot repeat too often—see that hands and mind are occupied. Despite the normal disabilities and discomforts which they have along with their contemporaries, busy useful old folks are rarely grumblers.

Many old people become greatly concerned about what happens to and with and inside their bodies. Although the saga, "My Operation," is not of course exclusively related by the elderly, the fact remains that the older people grow the more inclined they are to think about bodily processes. These, they are aware, have altered somewhat; they are fearful of further alterations and of becoming ill and helpless. Such anxieties are not entirely unreasonable with advancing age. But they are greatly intensified with idleness, so if your parent has a tendency to be preoccupied with the state of his health—and here we go again!—the best way to counteract it is to help him to busy himself in a worthwhile way.

There are also some practical measures which can assuage undue concentration on bodily functions. For instance, since increased frequency of urination is usual with advancing age, your parent will be less preoccupied with his need to "get up during the night" if the way to a nearby bathroom is kept lighted; or, if no toilet is convenient, a vessel should be kept handy in his room. Also, changing from one position to another becomes increasingly difficult with age. You will hear less about your parents' "stiffness" or "aching bones" and they will be less conscious of them if, rather than having no chairs except low-slung ones from which they can extricate themselves only with great effort, you take pains to provide one or two from which they can rise without longing for a derrick.

A familiar feature of old age is poor memory, and it may be just as normal for your parents to forget where they put their spectacles or false teeth or the registered letter for which they helpfully signed as it is for them to move slowly or not hear well. Nothing you do can restore the better memory of younger years. But you can circumvent your parents' present forgetfulness and so spare both yourself and them many occasions for embarrassment or vexation. Don't rely upon them to think of things. If you want to leave an instruction with them, write it out. If you don't want to miss telephone messages that come when you are not at home, be sure to have a pad and pencil at the telephone.

Related to the forgetfulness of age is the repetitiousness which makes sons and daughters groan, "If only Mom didn't tell the same story ten times over" or "Must he remind me again?" In part, saying the same thing many times is a means of getting attention, so an obvious alleviation—though no guaranteed remedy—is, as much as practicable, to avoid letting your parent feel by-passed. A new audience, as we said in Chapter 7 when we discussed the advantages for an old person in living with someone not his child; admiration for narratives which may be really interesting the first or even the second time they are heard, but not the twelfth, can be helpful in cutting down the number of times children must listen to "the same old thing." Or, if your parent lives with you, you might be able to get out of listening and please him at the same time by saying,

"Dad, do tell that story about your fishing trip to Canada to Mr. and Mrs. Jones while I'm in the kitchen (or putting away the car)."

Perhaps most tedious for those in much contact with the aged is their tendency to be circumstantial; that is, like some younger bores, garrulously to go into minute detail after detail. Adequate reproduction of talk of this kind would fill several pages of this book, but anyone who has ever heard it will know what we mean when we say that without focus it goes on and on from one point of association to another until the point of what the speaker started out to say is virtually lost. Much long-windedness comes from the desire to make an impression by those who know no other way to do it but to talk and talk and talk. Some garrulity, like repetitiousness, is a bid for attention.

As your parents' general abilities lessen it is highly important for you to concentrate on what they can do and as much as possible to ignore what they cannot. This very attitude, on your part, will help them healthfully to keep on doing. Your mother's eyesight may not be equal to the fine sewing she did formerly, nor may her legs and feet be up to walking to market, yet she may still be able to sit in the kitchen and peel fruit for preserving. Your father, with a good head for figures—although both you and he know that at eighty-four working daily in an office would be too much—might still assist you and your friends with income-tax calculations; or, if he was a mechanic, he may be able to advise or perhaps lend a hand when house and garden gadgets act up in your own or neighbors' homes. To housewives whose husbands are away in military service or on business, he could even become a kind of neighborhood hero.

The very same recognition, by you or others, of the fact that "Your parent is old," indeed "very old," has the potentiality of being either a source of pride or resentment. If he feels useless and dependent it will have a painful connotation. But if he feels helpful, a contributor, it can be a kind of compliment: "At your age, it's remarkable what you do," or even, "With what you do I can't quite believe you're that old!"

Although some evidences of aging occur in nearly everyone who lives long enough, and though, unlike youth, age itself is not curable, it will be important for your parent to have a check-up by a physician and a dentist at least once a year. Annual examinations, desirable at any age, are particularly so for the elderly because in them the line between health and sickness narrows to a point where it is difficult for anyone but a doctor to recognize when it is crossed. Detection and treatment of something that is just beginning to go wrong can save a deal of trouble later on and "An ounce of prevention is worth a pound of cure" is as true as it is trite.

This bit about annual check-ups goes for you, too, if you are forty or over! Maybe you have always been careless about health precautions. Maybe you figure that now your children are on their own so it isn't too important that you stay fit to take care of them. But if you have taken the trouble to read our book this far, you do feel responsibility for your aging parents, and it is highly important that you remain able to take care of them. No matter how well you feel or function, not to report to your doctor regularly once you have reached middle life is equivalent to not checking your gas, oil, and water before you start off on a long trip without knowing how far off the next service station may be.

Of course it would be fine if your parent (or you) could go to one of the geriatricians who are concerned with aging as pediatricians are concerned with infancy and childhood. But there are still only relatively few such specialists. The most essential qualifications for your parents' physician are that he know and understand your mother or father as a person, that he is medically familiar with their basic condition in case of acute illness, and that they like and respect him. The Mott family made the mistake, initially, of forcing upon their mother their own thirty-three-year-old physician, Dr. Haverford. But although he had excellent training, a fine reputation, and a competent, confident manner, old Mrs. Mott considered him "a young whippersnapper" too inexperienced to know what he was doing. "If I tell your mother to use an icebag, she thinks it ought to be a hot-water bag, and vice versa," Dr. Haverford told the children. "Do let me recommend an older man in whom she'll have confidence." The elder Mrs. Mott's new doctor was a portly graybeard who immediately won her approval and when he gave almost the identical recommendations about regimen which she had rejected from Dr. Haverford she accepted and followed them to her health's benefit.

Whenever you note any marked change in your parent's condition, seek medical help promptly. Recovery from even minor illnesses is slower in old folks than in younger ones, and reaction to accidents or infection more severe. Some children—and the aging parents concerned—rather have the idea that it is foolish to "bother with" or "spend a lot of money on" medical care for an old person, on the same theory on which one would not go in for extensive repairs on a very old house which could never be made good as new. Too many physicians, indeed, have the attitude, "What can you expect, at that age?" But don't overlook the fact that medical care isn't a matter of all or nothing. Even though your parent's sixty- or seventy- or eighty-year-old body admittedly can't be restored to the vigorous state it was in decades before, alleviation of aches and pains and impediments to activity can be vital to happiness. Your father's backache may not ever wholly disappear, but a little backache is much less uncomfortable and incapacitating than a big one. Your mother's arthritic hand may never again be truly flexible but if with treatment it can at least be used enough for her to brush her hair herself and turn down her bed, she is that much removed from complete helplessness.

The elimination of small discomforts perhaps not serious in themselves may also eliminate irritability. A dentist has an important regular place in your parent's health program. This holds even if your parent no longer has any of his own teeth. As the years go on, gums may shrink, and what were once well-fitted dentures become uncomfortable or fail properly to do their work of biting and chewing. A chiropodist (in some places called podiatrist), too, can be a valuable aide. No one in nagging distress from an ingrown toenail or corns or the wrong kind of shoes is likely to be cheerful or amiable, or inclined to be active, or apt to take the walks which are both physically and psychologically desirable, especially as we grow older.

In short, prompt, consistent medical and allied care, both preventive and remedial, though it may not produce the dramatic betterment in your parent as the same amount of effort and expense applied to someone younger, can nevertheless be crucial to his relative comfort and contentment.

These can also be furthered by a number of small adaptations of things and ways of living.

22

FOR THEIR SAFETY AND COMFORT

WITH COMMON SENSE and consideration, you can see that the surroundings in which your parents live and the hygiene of their daily life give them a certain desirable amount of protection yet do not destroy their sense of independence. Just as you can manage to stay adequately dry in the rain by using an umbrella and don't have to swathe yourself from head to foot in waterproof material, so can you take steps to safeguard your parents without acting as if you had to wrap them in cotton wool.

The main thing for you to keep in mind is that with aging there is both a physical and a psychological slowdown. Planning for safety and comfort should be geared not only to the disabilities of today but to the prevention of their intensification tomorrow. The regular medical examinations we have recommended will give the best answers as to what is all right for your parents to do and what isn't. For instance, does your father still see well enough to drive a car, or ought he to stop doing so now? Is your mother's heart in good enough shape so that it won't hurt her to climb stairs?

Generally, because old people don't move about with the ease of the young; because, at best, old bones take a long, long time to heal when broken, it is plain good sense not to invite home accidents. Falling is particularly dangerous for the aged. In 1961, of the 11,800 Americans who had fatal falls, 10,100 were sixty-four or more years old! Whether your parents live in your home or theirs, as we pointed out in Chapter 3, it ought to have no highly waxed floors or unanchored scatter rugs. Lamp cords ought not to lie across the floor or anywhere they are likely to become entangled around the feet of someone who has to move a chair to get to a desk or table. Stairways and outside steps should be well lighted, contain no broken or unsteady steps, and be provided with handrails in good repair.

There should be a handrail at the bathtub and a rubber mat to cover its slippery bottom. Advise your mother or father to have the bath fully drawn before getting into it to avoid the danger of dozing or fainting while hot water is still running. A stool in the bathroom on which to sit while undressing or dressing or drying, though not essential to safety, is pleasant for comfort.

Remove poisons from the medicine closet and kitchen shelves, not, unless your parent has grown very fuzzy with age, because you don't think he has the sense to know they are dangerous, but because poor eyesight may make him mistake one bottle for another. If you have a gas stove without a pilot light, watch it, because Mother may turn on the gas with the intention of making herself a cup of tea and then forget to light the burner. Be especially careful to have pot and pan handles turned inward whenever they are in use, lest your parent fumblingly or absentmindedly bump into one which is protruding, overturn the vessel, and be scalded. If your parent is going to use any new appliance, be sure to explain and demonstrate it first.

An unsteady bedside table can be a real hazard for an old person, who may use it as a brace for getting in and out of bed. If it topples over, he may fall too. Have a night light—there are small, ingenious ones to plug into wall outlets—anywhere your parents are likely to go in the dark. It will give reassurance as well as illumination.

Any part of the house which is what safety experts call a "traffic lane" should be kept clear of furniture so that your mother or father can pass through it with ease. Youngsters and all male members of the family will have to make a small sacrifice if Grandma or Grandpa lives in the same house and is going to be safe; they will have to overcome their predilection for leaving toys, rubbers, shoes, tools, magazines, and newspapers anywhere and everywhere on the floor, for "stumbling over small objects" is a major cause of home accidents. The lady of the house, although probably already a picker-upper, might also have to make a mildly painful adjustment to an aging parent by cutting rearrangements of the furniture to a minimum. It is even more disturbing to an old person than it is to a husband when things are moved out of their accustomed place. Not only might his slowed-down physical adjustment lead him to stumble over something which stands where there was empty space before, but also his slowed-down psychological adjustment makes the unfamiliar setup vaguely troubling.

Once you have become home-safety-conscious for your parents' sake, you will probably find many other ways you can cut down the chances of their having an accident without cutting down their mobility and freedom. Every safety feature you introduce and hazard you remove will benefit not only the old people but also all the other members of the household.

If your parent is not living in an apartment or a one-story house, or does not have a first-floor bedroom, once he comes downstairs for the day try to have what he may need at hand, so that he neither feels dependent on anyone to fetch for him nor has to make trips upstairs. Even if there is no medical prohibition on stair climbing, it may be an effort for an older person. If your parent is very old, you are probably well enough along yourself in age not to dash as unthinkingly up the stairs for any little thing as you did formerly, and you'll know what we mean.

Personal hygiene for the aged is not quite the same as for their juniors. Not only does it become unnecessary for them to bathe as often, but also daily baths are undesirable. With aging all bodily secretions diminish, and along with the advantage of lessened body odors goes the disadvantage of drier skin. Your parents ought to use a mild soap, and if the water where they live is hard, a water softener.

When it comes to clothing, your parent ought to be allowed to stick to his own way of dressing, whether it be based on woolens or nylons. Bearing in mind the tendency of old people to be chilly, be sure that winter coats are good and warm and that even for housewear your mother's or father's wardrobe includes sweaters or stoles or jackets. Your mother perhaps, ought not to wear round garters, which can be bad for circulation; if girdles are not for her, suggest a garter belt. Both men and women should have well-fitting, well-supporting shoes, preferably with rubber heels as a preventive of slipping.

The kind of bed in which your parents sleep should accord with former habits. Some old couples would be miserable with a double bed, and some with twin beds. A narrow day bed may suit your parent's taste better than a huge testered four-poster, or vice versa. Generally, a happy medium of a bed is desirable—one not so high that he'll hurt himself by falling out of it, nor so low that it's a struggle to get up. If, when he sits on the bed, his feet touch the floor, it should be about right for him, so if you are buying a new bed, correlate its height with your parent's. Usually the firmer a mattress, the better for an old person, but if he prefers a soft one, let him have it. A little pillow which can be tucked at the back of the neck or the small of the back or under the knee of a leg which hurts can be a big comfort.

Although old folks need fresh air as much as anybody else does, their tendency to chill makes getting up in a cold room even more of an ordeal for them than for the rest of us. If your mother or father lives with you, it might be an affectionate little service for one of your children to volunteer to shut Grandma's or Grandpa's window each morning. A hot drink in bed will help to get the day's routines started.

If your parent has a tendency to sleep fitfully, there is nothing alarming in it, as it is characteristic of the aged. Also, old people have a tendency to doze during the day. Make it possible for your parents to take little snoozes without their being put in an embarrassing situation. But if they seem to sleep most of the time it's probably an indication that they haven't enough to do, so try to find something that will keep them more awake.

Most old people appreciate having footstools at their chairs. But a show of proffering cushions when they sit down, however kindly its motives, only calls attention to their disabilities. The same is true of fussing about avoiding drafts, keeping your parents in when it rains, telling them they ought to take a rest, and the thousand and one affectionate, annoying ways of pointing out "you are old" which can be dreamed up by an oversolicitous child. If Grandma would rather become chilled than miss watching your son play football, or Grandpa prefers to have an aching back from cutting the lawn on a hot day rather than see it stay unkempt because the yard boy didn't come, the pleasures and pains are likewise rightfully theirs.

Exaggerated safety precautions for an aging parent can be as bad as none. Take, for instance, the way the four Baker sons and daughters devotedly destroy their mother. Although there is excellent bus service where she lives, she is never allowed to set foot in a public conveyance; someone will always manage to drop whatever he or she is doing to take Mama by car. A daughter or daughter-in-law invariably goes with her to shop or to a movie. And the upshot is that although Mrs. Baker is well and still physically vigorous for her years, emotionally she might as well be in a wheel chair, for she has actually become afraid to take a step by herself.

Although the Bakers' performances are extreme, many a son and daughter discourages or forbids an aged parent's going out for a stroll alone. Walks are desirable for old people for several reasons: they afford exercise, fresh air, and a change of scene. A walk alone, in addition, creates the possibility of making new contacts, and you ought neither to insulate nor overprotect your parent into dependence by insisting that someone must always be along when he goes for a stroll. Even if he is very feeble it is doubtful whether he will be in any serious danger by himself. Be sure he is well acquainted with the area where he walks, show him bad crossings and caution him about them, make sure that he carries identification, and then breathe easy when he is out. Somehow or other, passers-by always seem even more ready to help an old person get safely across the street than they are to help children, while automobile drivers who ordinarily act as if they were hell-bent on the murder of pedestrians practically always slow up to give an old man or woman right of way—even against the lights.

Similarly, encourage your parents to travel alone if they wish. Let their doctor, not your worries about them, determine whether it is still safe for them to drive. Escorted to the gate of their plane or seat of their bus or train at one end, and met at the other; with drivers, conductors and porters to help them in connection with trains, stewardesses and airline agents with airplanes, and fellow passengers likely to be helpful, really nothing much can happen to them. Certain trains have special hostesses aboard. It is possible to arrange in advance with airlines to have someone met by a special airline representative who will arrange for mechanized transportation or a wheel chair from the landing field to the baggage counter should the walk there be overlong for the traveler.

Even if your parents can afford first-class plane fare or Pullman, they may prefer traveling by coach or bus because they are afraid of flying or sleep more comfortably in reclining chairs than in berths, and if this is what they want to do, let them do it. A hike through a jolting train to reach a diner, or getting in and out of a bus to eat may present a problem, so food can be taken from home or brought to the passenger for a reasonable extra charge. A familiar little pillow taken along may add to comfort, too, although on all passenger airplanes and most trains going any considerable distance pillows are available.

In every aspect of your parents' life at home and abroad, see that they are not hurried. Remember that old people move and accommodate themselves relatively slowly and it is hard on them to be taken to terminals on split-second timing, to have to rush through their toilet and bath or leap out of bed to get somewhere. But slowing down is not cessation, so do not thicken what should be a mere veneer of precaution and protection until it is tantamount to a coffin.

The tendency for children to be overprotective, while it may affect the quality of the job of caring for aging parents in respect to diet, is not as great a hazard as another one which is likely most of all to involve the lady of the house, whether she does the cooking herself or supervises it. It is the difficulty of being dispassionate about food.

23

DIFFICULTIES WITH DIET

WHETHER OR NOT you and your parents live together, the matter of how well they are eating is going to be on your mind. This concern with food is filial and right. Since food is essential to life itself it has more profound emotional implications than almost any other aspect of daily life. Throughout the ages the deep meaning of food has been recognized by its inclusion in religious ceremonies and the significance put upon such acts as "breaking bread."

The provision of food is such an elemental part of living that if your parent criticizes what is offered it is almost like criticism of you, and the feelings aroused go much deeper than a difference of opinion about the amount of pepper in the soup or the point at which a roast becomes overdone. Any stresses and strains which arise in connection with meals are not only more intense than is apparent in what is said, but also are twofold, because your feelings as well as your parents' feelings are involved.

Understanding and good management of the emotional as well as the physical aspects of diet can, however, considerably reduce "fussing and feuding" over food.

There is no reason to be disturbed if your parent's appetite is changeable and eventually so small that "it wouldn't keep a bird alive," for you can expect this to happen. To some extent it is caused by the decrease in the senses of taste and smell which we discussed in Chapter 18, but there are other contributing causes.

Since physical activity usually lessens in the later years older people do not need as much food as younger ones and are therefore less hungry. Lack of interest in eating may be part of a general loss of interest in living and lack of enthusiasm for anything. Dislike of certain foods, although your parent may not be conscious of any tie-in with digestibility, may accord with what doesn't too well agree with him. Toothlessness or ill-fitting dentures are another appetite-dampener.

Here again your parent may not realize, and will probably not admit, why he doesn't enjoy eating; he is more likely to blame the quality, flavor, or selection of the food than his disabilities. Even when dentures fit well, since they are no perfect replacement of natural teeth, certain foods such as berries and figs, which contain small seeds that get under the dentures, are eaten with discomfort. Biting with false teeth on raw celery, radishes, corn on the cob, whole apples, and perhaps even lettuce requires deliberate effort, so unless your parent is especially fond of these foods he may not find their consumption worth the struggle. Since you can always manage to find substitutes with the same food values the issue isn't worth the battle, so let your mother or father get away with "don't like" or "isn't good" when it's really "can't chew."

More subtly underlying a finicky appetite is the glamour surrounding the food known in childhood. Lothar Schultz, once a boy immigrant from Germany, for years had impressed his American-born children with the superior quality, size, color, and flavor of the fruits grown in his native village; nothing produced in this country, he insisted, could equal them. Having amassed a tidy sum by his sixties, he treated the whole family to a trip back to his birthplace, and when he actually saw the small, unremarkable fruit he had for so long been idealizing, his chagrin was equaled only by his sons' and daughters' ill-concealed amusement.

Unfortunately, most aging parents cannot be similarly confronted with the evidence, so they continue to compare the unreal glories of a past diet with the realities of their present one. If you are a daughter, you may go through again what you suffered when you were a bride—invidious comparisons with "what Mother used to make." Only this time, and even harder to debunk, the perfect cooking will have been your grandmother's long ago.

If your mother or father lives alone, it is quite proper for you to keep a watchful eye on her or his diet. Even the best proponents of live-alone-and-like-it theories, whatever their age, are liable to let down on balancing their meals by eating whatever is most easily prepared. With an older person, the effort of shopping for food and lugging it home is an additional discouragement to varied and abundant diet. It may be necessary for you to see that your parent receives a good many invitations to eat out, or for you tactfully to take over meals now and then, as we suggested in Chapter 3.

Although lack of eating is one problem with older people, eating too much may be another. Usually the ones who sit and overeat are those who don't have anything else to do, who are unhappy, who find their only satisfaction in stuffing themselves. The dangers of obesity are much publicized and well known these days, and few of us need to be told that overweight, although a strain on the heart in particular, increases the seriousness of any disease. If your parent eats overmuch, you cannot solve the problem by scoldings and hiding food. What he needs are interests and satisfactions.

It may be that your mother or father requires a special diet, as for a diabetic or kidney condition. This, of course, should be individually prescribed by a physician. But all old people ought to follow certain fairly simple general principles of eating. Many difficulties previously ascribed to old age are now known to come from improper diet.

Proteins should be increased, and carbohydrates—starch and sugar—and fats decreased. Animal proteins, like those in lean meat, milk, cheese, and eggs, are preferable to those in vegetables like beans. Although it is ordinarily not necessary to go to such extremes as cutting out the normal amount of butter or margarine served at table, foods fried in deep fat, desserts rich in cream and sugar, cakes and pastries should be drastically cut down or, better still, eliminated. Fruits and vegetables are important, especially when, because of dental conditions, a diet largely soft or liquid is inadequate. Unless the doctor prescribes laxatives it is always better to depend upon diet than upon medication for the prevention of constipation.

The importance of vitamins in the diet of an aging person cannot be overstressed, and foods like liver and eggs, which are rich in Vitamin B, should have a high priority. Here again, as in the matter of roughage, foods, not pills, should be depended on to supply what is needed unless your parent's physician prescribes supplementary vitamins in concentrated form.

As long as the doctor does not advise to the contrary, it is quite all right for your parent to take the same amount of coffee or tea to which he has always been accustomed. Give him the seasoning which pleases him, and don't, except under doctor's orders, deprive him of tobacco or alcohol.

Now if your parent has never been much of a one for heavy, rich, greasy foods, has always been a meat and egg eater, and has long preferred fruits or cheese to sweet baked desserts, you won't have much trouble getting him to adapt his eating to his years. But if the diet suitable for an old person is entirely different from what he has always had and liked, getting him accustomed to it won't be easy on either of you. It is hard for anyone to change lifelong eating habits, hardest for the old who have had them so long fixed. Also, let us remind you again what deep and complex feelings are associated with food.

Gradually wean your parents into a new way of eating. If they have been accustomed to large meals, don't jolt, but ease them into having smaller ones, for with aging fewer calories are needed to keep going. Little by little, so that it isn't strikingly evident, reduce fats and sweets. In an unobvious way, go easier and easier on servings of bread and potatoes. Every now and then slip in fruit desserts before you establish them as a regular replacement for cakes and pies. It won't always be smooth going because, after all, a banana can't ever be the same as a banana pie, but you may be sure the going will be much rougher if you are abrupt. Also, you will have less trouble if you put the emphasis on "This is what you like" rather than "This is good (or not good) for you."

Large amounts of food at a time may be overpowering for old people, so it may be preferable to provide your parents with small amounts of nourishment given five times a day rather than the usual three meals. Of course you will have to fit this kind of service somehow into your family schedule, and at in-between times you may find it more convenient to serve nourishing beverages like eggnogs than regular sit-down meals. It is desirable, however, that your parents get their food with some regularity.

Preserve your aging parents' sense of dignity by trying to serve as unobtrusively as possible specially prepared foods like ground meats and puréed vegetables. If you must use canned baby foods—which will probably be despised as "pap"—do your best to keep their containers invisible.

Even if your parent's diet has to be quite different from the rest of the family's, he ought not to eat by himself, except, perhaps, for taking breakfast in his room. Mealtimes are a social as well as nutritional matter, so don't accept any well-meant offers on your mother's or father's part to "just have a tray by myself." It furthers a sense of well-being in general and digestion in particular to eat with others, and the old, like everyone else, benefit by mealtime companionship and conversation. But old people should never be hurried through their meals; the atmosphere in which they eat ought to be leisurely. It may indeed be salutary for the whole family to have to set their tempo at table in accord with Grandma's or Grandpa's.

For your own sake as well as your parents', don't let yourself become too involved with what and how much they eat. Again we caution about the hurts, worries, and tensions liable to arise in connection with food, which can become troubling out of all apparent proportion to disputes over a teaspoon of salt, lemon omitted in a sauce, or a serving too large or too small. If you see that your father or mother have reasonably good, properly balanced food in a pleasant atmosphere you are doing your job as well as anyone can.

If your parent has always been a normally alert, amiable person, and seems to be becoming apathetic or irritable, it is wise to check with the doctor, because sometimes—though not always—such behavior is an early symptom of very mild nutritional deficiency. Its chief danger lies in its starting a vicious cycle of lack of interest in eating and consequently more severe deficiency and still less desire to eat.

For the same reason you need to be keenly aware of dietary needs in times of illness or convalescence. Then your aging parent, more knocked out by small sicknesses than a younger person would be, also has more edge off what may already be a small appetite, and his not eating well may retard recovery.

But in any case, no matter how carefully your parent's health is guarded, the older he grows, the less chance there is that he will escape being sick in bed for shorter or longer periods.

PART VI

If They Are Sick or Disabled

24

ACUTE ILLNESS

IT GOES WITHOUT saying that you hope your mother or father won't become sick or disabled. But like everything else we have talked about in this book, the possibility—indeed probability—of their being bedfast and of resultant problems, is something for which it is well to be psychologically prepared. There is a happy medium between anxiously awaiting and expecting Mom or Dad to fail and being too blithely unaware that they could ever become seriously incapacitated. Strike it and you will neither fret about a dismal future and overprotect your parents into hastening it, nor, when sickness does come will you meet it with the shock and protest which are the usual reactions to unforeseen calamity.

There are two general categories of severe illness: acute, or short-term, and chronic, or long-term. Sometimes there may be a flare-up of a long-term illness and for a period it becomes acute. Naturally you will deal with acute illness in a parent as you would with anyone else close to you. A doctor or doctors, nursing care, medication and perhaps transient hospitalization will be involved. Like acute illness in any other member of your family it will temporarily upset your household and personal schedules and very likely it will dominate your thoughts until it is over, for better or for worse.

If he has to go to a hospital for a while, however, you may not realize the terror the very word "hospital" generates in some old people, especially if they have never been hospitalized before. Your mother may have had her babies at home and your father been nursed through pneumonia or typhoid fever right in his own bed. When many of today's old people were young they thought of a hospital as a place where you went to die and now these childhood fears may be reactivated. Do everything you possibly can to reassure them as anxiety and tension can greatly impede their recovery. If the situation is not an emergency one take them to see the inside of the hospital before it is time for them to be admitted so that it will not be totally strange. Avoid letting your own pessimism, if you feel it, show through. This does not mean that you should burble with silly optimism that inevitably will not ring true, but simply that you should maintain a cheerful, valid attitude of hopefulness.

Transmitting such an attitude is perhaps most important—and most difficult!—if your parent is going to have an operation. Few of us old enough to be concerned about an aging parent realize the marvelous advances in surgery, anesthesiology, and internal medicine which have reduced the risks of operations on even the very, very old. If you go on the assumption that your parent's chances, whatever his age, of recovering after surgery are just about as good as if he were younger, you will be fooling neither yourself nor him but acting sensibly on the basis of proven medical fact.

Sometimes a surgeon asks a family which kind of surgery they would prefer to have him perform: drastic, with a good possibility of thoroughgoing correction of a condition; or palliative, involving much less pain, upset, and inconvenience for the aged patient. Frequently, sons and daughters insist upon the former with the idea that anything less would not be doing right by Mom or Dad. Avoid letting any uneasiness that you might feel guilty if you did not sanction the more thoroughgoing operation keep you from deciding upon the one which can relieve your parent without his being put through so much.

If one of your parents becomes ill, it may give some ease of mind to the other to know that there is a medical aid to the aged program whereby federal funds assist the states to make hospital care available to aged persons of low income. This same knowledge may also lessen your own anxiety as to how the cost of your parent's acute illness might be met, and leave you freer to comfort both patient and spouse. Ask your local Department of Welfare for information on your state's eligibility requirements and provisions for medical aid to the aged.

When your mother or father is home from the hospital—their home or yours—like all convalescents, they are likely to be more than usually irritable, and even more than younger ones, to be demanding. During times of illness and weakness the old have a special fear of being deserted and greatly need assurance and reassurance of family interest. Frequent visits, gifts, telephone calls, greeting cards, and any other little attentions favorably influence not only their spirits but also their actual recovery. It is not an undue strain to be attentive, even appeasing, when there is a happy ending in sight. But long-term sickness or disability is something else.

25

CARING FOR THEM AT HOME

WHILE YOUR MOTHER or father is acutely ill your filial emotions are probably intense, and you certainly do not need us to remind you to care for him or her well. But—and few of us admit this even to ourselves—quite another matter are the prolonged convalescences of the aged, as, to an even greater degree, are long-term illnesses. The first fine flush of love and devotion tends to pale as weeks or months or years pass by. The patience of both invalid and the well members of the family becomes sorely tired. Along with the lessening of hope for complete recovery comes an increasing sense of "What's the use?"—drab and depressing in comparison with the drama of short-term efforts to "get him on his feet again." Make no mistake about it, it is going to be hard on everyone concerned if your parent, like so many old folks today, is incapacitated by long-term illness for a considerable period.

If arrangements can be made for your parent to be cared for in his home, and remaining there is what he prefers, by all means let him do so. In Chapter 3 we have already given suggestions as to enlisting homemakers, visiting nurses, and home health aides. These still hold good if illness comes, but now we are thinking about more severe disabilities and serious sickness, so we want to add others.

An increasing, but still inadequate, number of hospitals provide "coordinated home care" for long-term aged patients, even with such serious conditions as terminal cancer or paralyzing strokes. If you can arrange for this for your parent in your community either in his own or your home, he is indeed fortunate. With such care the patient gets just about everything he could get in the less cozy and familiar atmosphere of the hospital itself—medical supervision, nursing, occupational therapy, physical therapy with the loan of apparatus if necessary, social work and homemaker service. It is only fair to warn you that with the shortage of personnel probably old people with no living relatives get priority; nevertheless, anything you might utilize to help your parent stay at home, his or yours, rather than go to an institution, is worth trying to get.

But even if your invalided parent lives with you without hospital-sponsored coordinated home care, his presence, while disturbing, need not cast a pall over your household. The more help you get from professionals skilled and experienced in dealing with sickness, the less disruptive your parent's illness will be for himself and you and your family. Your knowledge of even such apparently trivial procedures as how to make a bed with a patient in it, how to lift or turn a person in bed, where and how to place pillows, and how to give a bed bath can not only make your parent more comfortable and contented, but also save you a great deal of fatiguing waste motion. You might, for instance, enroll in one of the home nursing courses given by the Red Cross or a Y. Visiting nurses will come in not only to give treatments requiring professional skill, such as injections, but also to instruct the family in the care of patients. Public health nurses in some rural communities do bedside nursing as well as teaching. Everywhere public health nurses are at your service for instruction. As their name implies, they are available to the public in general, not only to those unable to pay, and as a citizen you need not hesitate to call upon your local health department.

When your parents were young any family at all well-to-do would engage a "trained nurse" (on twenty-four-hour duty!) to look after its invalids. But even the wealthy may now have difficulty in obtaining the services of private-duty professional nurses (RN) for any extended period of home care. Today's licensed practical nurse (LPN) has as much training as the registered nurse of a generation or so ago and unless your parent has an especially complicated condition, she is qualified to give him good regular care. On the other hand, the old-fashioned "practical nurse" who did the housework in addition to looking after the patient has gone the way of a Model T Ford. Official registries for LPN's specify that their nurses will cook and clean only specifically for the patient. A nurses official registry will either have a listing of LPN's as well as of RN's or be able to tell you where to get one. If there is no nearby nurses official registry, inquire at your local department of health; do not take a chance with purely commercial registries which may call anybody a "nurse" in order to get a fee.

Avoid making the mistake of hasty acceptance of a temporary illness as permanent, and of the assumption that if your parent is very sick at an advanced age there is not much hope of his ever getting any better. There is no time of life at which some improvement is impossible and, as we pointed out in Chapter 21, medical care and treatment, though they may not be one hundred per cent effective, are never entirely useless. Even in the most fixed and long-term illnesses in the very old, almost daily ups and downs may be expected. Sons and daughters do well to emulate the policy of the better homes for the aged, which are very flexible in transferring residents back and forth from "ambulant" and "infirmary" sections.

The Morrison sons, for example, would have made a fatal mistake had they assumed their aged mother would become a permanent invalid. At eighty she sprained her back lifting a sewing machine—a mishap which brings to mind the old joke about grandfather's falling off his bicycle. The formerly alert and cheerful old lady had to take to her bed, and, while there, she developed a rather severe bronchial infection. This, combined with the length of time it took the sprain to heal, brought her spirits down to an all-time low, and for the first time "the boys," aged fifty and fifty-five, began to wonder whether this mightn't be the beginning of the end. Fortunately, however, they managed to maintain a cheerful and encouraging attitude, and ultimately Mrs. Morrison was up and about again. Today, on the eve of her eighty-fifth birthday, she is hoping to get enough birthday money to buy a new fur coat, and during the past year she has happily sortied from her home in New York to visit one of the sons in Michigan and the other in Maryland.

Use any upturn in your parent's health for all it is worth and for just as long as it lasts. Too many devoted sons and daughters have a tendency to discourage sick and aging parents from taking advantage of days or weeks or months of relative good health for fear a setback will result. Actually there is no reason for any child to reproach himself should the always see-sawing health of an aged mother or father suffer after what might have been too much activity. For one thing, the setback might have occurred anyway. For another, the philosophy embodied in "Gather ye rosebuds while ye may" and *carpe diem* is even more appropriate for the old than for the young, whose monopoly it is usually considered. The old do not have as many days left to enjoy.

Bearing this in mind, you will not, except under doctor's orders, keep in bed a mother or father who has been sick or has had a worsening of a long-term condition merely for fear that getting up might be harmful. Nor, except under doctor's orders, will you deny the joy of having company to the sociable kind of man or woman who loves it. Your parent, although very ill, may even welcome visits from grandchildren or great-grandchildren. To you the idea of a sickroom invasion, even briefly, by noisy, chattering, restless small fry may be appalling. But never forget that to your mother or father the children's liveliness may represent life rather than annoyance. In any case, in the last analysis, even if desired company turns out to be fatiguing, the worst that can happen is that a long life might be shortened by a few days.

If your parent has been paralyzed by a stroke, or crippled by arthritis, avoid thinking about him in terms of permanent incapacity. With his doctor's guidance explore rehabilitative facilities in your community. Seeming miracles have been wrought by physicians, physical therapists, speech therapists, occupational therapists, nurses, psychologists, and social workers, proceeding as a team, in restoring "done for" old people. Nowadays strokes, for example, need not be the dread permanent cripplers which fill inferior nursing homes. It is important to start rehabilitation immediately. Then, with skilled professional direction of exercise, treatment, and activity, some perhaps with elaborate specialized apparatus but much, also, with ordinary household equipment, the effects of strokes may be overcome in a matter of weeks.

But "rehabilitation," we must warn you, may not always mean that your parent will be independent and self-sufficient again. This he may well be, but it is rehabilitation if he is able to walk after having been bedfast; if he is able to speak intelligibly after he has lost all power to speak; or even if, after having been incontinent, he is able to attend to his bathroom needs. So talk with your physician and look up Rehabilitation in your telephone directory, or inquire at your local hospitals as to what rehabilitative services for out-patients they may have, or call your local health department. Not to take advantage of whatever rehabilitative services may be available to your aging parent would be like not having taken advantage of local educational services for your children.

Precisely as with aging people who are well, the hazards of the sick and smitten doing too little are greater than the hazards of their doing too much. No matter how ill your parent becomes it is important for him to have the greatest possible range of interests and activities, for even within the narrow limits of a bed, a bed-room, an apartment, or a house, there is no need for anyone merely to mark time until death. Exercise all your ingenuity to find con-genial pursuits and occupations for your bedfast or housebound parent. A few suggestions about what has been done by and for some invalided old folks will, we hope, start you off on other ideas of your own.

Mr. Hartman, for instance, homebound for many years by cardiac asthma, interested himself in cultivating the friendship of the squir-rels which scurried about the grounds of his suburban house. Un-able to go any further than the porch, he would lure them with food; and he brought them to such a point of confidence that they would perch on his knees and shoulders. When a female he had named Bushy had babies, and a male he called Harry was murdered by a neighbor's dog, these were major events in Mr. Hartman's circumscribed life.

Bedfast Mr. Elbertson liked birds, so his daughter-in-law put a feeding station outside his window and the old man spent hours identifying and noting in his tremulous old-fashioned script the various species which availed themselves of its hospitality. Mrs. Glover spent hours watching the doings of the tropical fish in an aquarium in her room. Plants, though less active than animals, are more interesting than cut flowers, which can only be looked at until they die. African violets or philodendron or any plants which do well in the house might be something for your parent to watch change and grow and, if he is able to make the effort, to tend.

Of course if your father or mother has always been a reader and eyesight is still adequate, you have an endless resource in the nearest circulating or public library and can supplement TV with whole worlds in printed pages. Even if vision is gone, your library may be able to get you "talking books." Capitalize on any special interests. Mr. Rawlings, a lawyer, asked his father, a retired lawyer, to clip for him from the *Law Journal*. A daughter asked her mother to keep a weather eye out for good recipes.

Many invalids enjoy handwork. Mrs. Pemberton, bedfast for fifteen years, turned out fifty patchwork quilts as presents for friends and family, and at eighty she was still going strong. Knitting, needlepoint, and crewel embroidery are other possibilities.

If you are so fortunate as to have in your community one of the handful of occupational therapists in private practice, either engage her to come in regularly or, if that is beyond your means, confer with her about what crafts might be suitable for your parents. If, as is probable, no private-practice occupational therapist is available, you might be able to get some help from one employed in a nearby hospital. Occupational therapists are not only familiar with a wide variety of crafts, but also have the medical background to know what would and what would not be suitable for someone in your parent's condition.

There is a real difference between "occupation" and "entertainment" for your parent. Many children's first and only thought about time-passers for a bedfast aging parent is "television" or "radio." True, these devices have made a vast difference in the lives of shut-ins, but as a kind of spectator sport; being glued to them is no substitute for the more active kind of doing which helps an old person to feel that he is still taking part in something.

The same goes for well-intended, sacrificial attempts continually to "amuse" Mother or Father. Often these end with the children either being virtually chained to a chair in the sickroom or feeling guilty when they are away from it to attend to housework or business. Much better for all concerned than head breaking over "What can I do to entertain Mom (or Dad)?" is "What can I find for them to entertain themselves?" The provision of materials for doing crossword and jigsaw puzzles, of hobbies, and of books and magazines is better than "entertainment" which, in overdoses, is sooner or later sure to pall.

Even a small change of scene may greatly improve the spirits and disposition of someone compelled to look at the same walls and ceiling most of the time. Unless sitting in a car is acutely uncomfortable for your parent, unless the doctor says when you ask him that it would not be good for your mother or father to go for a ride in the car, don't let your own apprehension that "Mom might catch cold" or "Dad would be exhausted" keep you from giving the pleasure and stimulation of occasional drives, not to where *you* would like to go but where he or she would. You, for example, who have been working in town all week would love to get out into the restful country, but Grandma may get more out of going down city streets so she can window-shop from the car, sense activity, and see crowds. There are seasonal treats in being taken to look at Christmas lights, spring or autumn foliage. Even a bedfast old person can be afforded some change of scene if he has one of the movable beds which can be bought from a dealer in hospital supplies. Such a bed can be wheeled out onto a porch or from one room to another. If there is room for it in the dining room, your parent might enjoy having his dinner there instead of alone in his room. Sometimes he might want to be in the midst of family life in the living room, and early Christmas morning when the packages are opened don't let worries about his "losing sleep" or "suffering from the noise" prevent you from letting him share in the fun and excitement.

It must be admitted that no matter how successful you are in helping your parent to lead some kind of life of his own, as an invalid his interests will inevitably narrow and he will tend to become more and more involved with his symptoms, aches, and pains. If it can be at all consonant with the truth, meet his complaints with encouraging remarks suggestive of progress: "I know, but look how much worse you felt day before yesterday" or "The attack you had last spring was much more severe, and then a few weeks later you were walking about again." If optimism would be ridiculously farfetched, about all you can do is try to divert your parent from thoughts of himself by giving him something to do and think about.

Just as our story is one of "interests and occupations for the aging" throughout this book, so it is one of "independence." And we stick to that now, too. Permit your parent to do everything for himself that he possibly can. Even if he is incurably paralyzed you will probably be able to save him from sinking into complete helplessness. If he is able to push his wheel chair, let him do so. Encourage him to get out of bed. Rig up a pulley system so that he need not ask for help in sitting up or turning. Keep within his reach anything he is likely to use, like a glass of water or magazines or his pills, so that he need not have to ask someone for every little thing he wants. If one side of his body is paralyzed, be sure to give him opportunities and motives for using the other. There are a wide variety of devices for helping the disabled to sit up, walk, go to the bathroom by themselves, take their own showers, use their hands. Ask your physician about these and see what is in a surgical supply store. The temptation to wait upon and serve someone largely incapacitated is very great, but you will have your reward for not succumbing to it from the continuing maintenance of your parent's self-respect and perhaps the very prolongation of a life he feels is still worth living.

You will not, of course, always be able to gauge just what your mother or father is able to do or by what means or devices they may be rendered less helpless, and here again you will find professional help invaluable. In addition to getting information from the doctor, consult a public health nurse or physical therapist who should have many tricks and techniques for encouraging self-help to pass on to you. A visit to a veterans' hospital, equipped with devices for paralytics and set up with facilities for helping them to help themselves, might send you home full of ideas for preserving the remnants of your parent's physical independence even if no local rehabilitation service is available to your parent.

Sickness and disability, albeit the patient is cared for at home, always bring additional expense. Help your parent to take advantage of any health insurance he may carry, and this includes the least well known of the social security benefits. Practically everyone knows that if he has made enough social security payments, after he is sixty-two he is entitled to some income. But surprisingly few people know of the disability benefits which social security payments also insure an eligible person less than sixty-five in the same amount as would be due at the later age. Your local Social Security Administration office can supply details of eligibility. Roughly, the disability must be so severe that the beneficiary is unable to earn a living. It must have lasted at least six months before benefits begin to be paid, and be of such a nature that it is expected to continue indefinitely. Examples of conditions ordinarily severe enough to qualify a person for disability benefits are loss of the use of two limbs through accident or disease; progressive, incurable cancer, and total hearing or speech loss which cannot be corrected.

Disability benefits may also be claimed for an eligible person with brain damage which has brought about severe loss of judgment, intellect or memory, and for mental diseases that require constant supervision of the patient. Mental and emotional disorders can occur at any time of life.

26

MENTAL AND EMOTIONAL DISORDERS

As PEOPLE OF ALL ages develop emotional disorders and psychiatric illnesses, similarly at all ages do they need treatment in keeping with their particular need. If your parent acts abnormally childlike or depressed or confused, or almost continuously does not know who or where he is, or his personality changes sharply, or he has delusions (fixed ideas contrary to the facts) or hallucinations (seeing, hearing, or smelling things which aren't there) do not put it down to "just old age," but get psychiatric evaluation.

Sympathetic, well-meaning, but uninformed friends may try to prevent you from making what they think are futile and perhaps expensive efforts to improve your parent's condition. Research, however, has demonstrated that sick minds and emotions are not caused by time in itself, but are the result of situations in which the aged find themselves, or of disease, or both. While these are not always preventable or correctible, with comprehensive and intensive treatment the chances of improvement or recovery are about the same for older mental patients as for any other age group.

Children tend to find it hard to face up to the fact of deterioration or aberration in a parent. For example, the sons and daughters of eighty-five-year-old Mrs. Granger, who was beginning to suffer from a disease affecting her brain, behaved as if she were the same self-sufficient old lady she had been until about two years before. When she could not remember what had been said to her a few minutes earlier, when she asked repeatedly what day it was or how many grandchildren she had now, when her former fastidious grooming changed into slovenliness, they excused her (and themselves from doing anything) with "Well, what can we expect at her age?" Not until she had no idea where she was when she was out alone one block from her home, and she frequently wet herself without bothering to change her clothes, did they realize something must be seriously wrong and seek psychiatric help.

At the other extreme, some adult children pounce on any and all minor evidences of forgetfulness or carelessness as "senility," a term as loosely overused as "neurotic." All of us are occasionally absent-minded or lose our way or fail to report telephone messages. If you constantly expect your aged parent to be mentally incompetent very likely it will not be long before he meets your expectations, and if you consider his "senility" hopeless, it will be.

Some psychiatric conditions in the old as well as the young can be treated in an outpatient community mental health clinic or the office of a psychiatrist in private practice. Some require treatment, care, and protection in a hospital, although not necessarily round-the-clock. There are a growing number of day hospitals, from which patients return home nightly, and of night hospitals, which permit patients to lead their usual lives during the day. Even if full-time hospitalization is recommended for your parent, he may not ever have to leave the community to go to a faraway state or private psychiatric hospital. More and more general hospitals are adding psychiatric services to their traditional services such as surgical or obstetric. Admission, no more complicated than to any other service, requires none of the commitment proceedings usually distressing to relatives, and the time spent in the hospital may be no longer than a month. Indeed, with medication to be continued after discharge, it can be as little as a week.

Possibly your parent will fail to improve during a short-term stay in a general hospital, or no community hospital takes psychiatric patients. Then, if his psychiatrist so advises, he should go to a mental hospital. It may be that only there can he get one or more of the various, specialized kinds of therapy which will remedy his disorder if it is remediable and ameliorate it if it is not: occupational, physical, drug, activity, electroshock, and group psychotherapy. It may be that if he is not under constant supervision he is dangerous to himself or others—but not primarily in the sense of "violence" which is quite rare. Danger lies also in the loss of will to live and of failure to eat, characteristic of depression; in the extreme absent-mindedness which may habitually cause your mother to turn on the gas to boil water for a cup of tea and then forget to light it or your father to thread his way diagonally through traffic oblivious of traffic lights and honking horns; in following the commands of "voices" or misidentifying a member of the family as a mortal enemy.

Yet despite the absolute rightness of hospitalizing an aged mental patient when doing so is necessary or desirable, there is an unfortunate widespread idea that the children of the men and women admitted to state hospitals for the first time at sixty-five or over, are delighted to be rid of a burden and have callously cast off their parents. Studies have shown that nothing could be further from the truth. Almost never do children have their parents committed without guilt, anguish, and honest attempts to find other means of care and treatment. You would be superhuman if you did not share something of the emotions whipped up by popular fallacy, but the more you can look upon hospitalization for your parent's broken judgment and memory and ability to reason in the same way as you would look upon it for broken bones, the less perturbed you will be. Visit soon after your parent is admitted and often throughout his stay unless you are told not to by his doctor or social worker. Write if distance prevents frequent visiting. In short, continue to show interest in your parent as you would if he were in a general hospital, and never worsen his condition by letting him feel abandoned. He may not recognize you or seem to understand what you say, but psychiatric experience has demonstrated that mental patients take in much more than their behavior indicates.

Even in the poorest mental hospital which is understaffed and offers little in the way of skilled, specialized treatment to its aged patients, your parent may recover or improve sufficiently to return home. Strange as the idea may seem, the atmosphere in mental hospitals is generally relaxing. Employees, accustomed to the idiosyncrasies of the mentally ill, are more easygoing and tolerant than most of the people your parent would encounter in the world outside—including the family! Fellow patients have foibles and weaknesses like himself, and he is not under pressure to compete with younger, clearer-thinking folk. Daily life is scheduled for him with regular times for rest and meals. Many aged patients quickly lose symptoms of what appears to be severe, long-term mental illness to a large extent because their health is built up with a nutritious, well-balanced diet.

Indeed, physical and mental health are interrelated. There are components of mental illness in almost every physical illness and components of physical illness in almost every mental illness. Most strokes, for example, have primarily physical effects. Yet after someone has suddenly found himself unable to move some part of his body, or to speak clearly, the shock, frustration, and worry, untreated, may be almost as devastating as the loss of muscular control itself, and he is doubly immobilized.

Depression is another example of the interrelationship of emotional and physical. Although depression may occur at any age, for several reasons it is commoner among the old than the young. If they have an accident or become sick it is harder for them to struggle back to their feet, and they are especially liable to be dejected if they have a setback after doing pretty well. Even if an old person is in relatively good physical health, he is vulnerable to despondency because—often with justice—he feels lonely or isolated or unwanted or without status in the community any more. Having lost interest in life he tends to be inactive, to the detriment of circulation, appetite, digestion, and sleep, and so his physical health suffers, which makes him all the more depressed. We could go on endlessly saying "and so because he is more depressed, his physical health suffers more, which makes him . . ." but the point is that whether physical or emotional ill health give the first push in a vicious circle of deterioration, unless there is skilled, understanding intervention, even an initially mild depression can bring about as an end product a helpless man or woman who requires constant supervision and care. Too often such a preventable unhappy ending to a long life is attributed to one of the less preventable, physiological diseases of the brain rarely striking under sixty, such as cerebral arteriosclerosis or senile brain disease.

If your seriously confused, forgetful, or irrational parent has sufficient property to make it worthwhile to protect him against his own inability to handle money, although it will probably hurt and disturb you to have him legally declared incompetent, you ought to see that this is done. As a rule a lawyer will attend to all the necessary proceedings without your having to participate in these in person, and the court will appoint a guardian (in some states called "conservator") to invest and disburse funds in your parent's interest.

Even if there is severe, irreparable brain damage, the principles of all we have said about the value of continuous medical-psychiatric supervision, occupation, stimulation of interests, and family relations hold true. As a person handicapped by partial vision or a missing limb can be helped to make the most of what he has left, so your seriously senile or arteriosclerotic parent can be helped to make the most of what is left of his mind and life. Toward this end a good mental hospital may be better than his own home, your home, or a nursing home.

On the other hand, under some circumstances a good nursing home might be the best possible place for your mother or father.

27

CARE IN A NURSING HOME

IF YOUR PARENT has an incapacitating chronic illness that does not require the constant presence of physicians on the premises, as in a hospital; or is physically handicapped to an extent where he needs skilled help in eating, bathing, or moving about; or requires nursing care during convalescence from an acute illness, surgery, or accident; or is mildly senile or arteriosclerotic and too confused to be able to carry on everyday activities; or has simply become so feeble and fragile with advanced age that he can do little or nothing for himself, it is likely to be primarily in his best interest and only secondarily in yours to find a suitable nursing home.

For one thing, there he can get the round-the-clock attention and knowledgeable care difficult or impossible to provide at home. For another, he may be helped to live longer and more comfortably with the comprehensive, coordinated, skilled nursing and rehabilitative services first-rate nursing homes provide. Their specialized equipment can also be a great asset. Just one example of this is a threshold-less shower with a door sufficiently wide for wheel chairs to roll in. Mrs. Levitt, whose daughter had been lovingly sponge-bathing her ever since she had become paralyzed from the waist down, sighed luxuriously when as a nursing-home patient she gave herself a wheel chair shower bath. "This is the first time in five years," she told a nurse, "that my whole body has been under water!"

We must tell you frankly, however, that when we speak of the possible advantages of a nursing home for your aged parent, we mean a nursing home in more than name. Unhappily, although public health officials and authorities on aging have long been working to define terms and set standards, too many so-called nursing homes remain no more than repositories for the sick and infirm aged. Care in a true nursing home is under the continuous expert supervision of professional nurses, who direct the work of licensed practical nurses and nurses' aides to the end of maintaining the patients' best possible health and morale. Since staff is the major item in nursing home budgets, such care cannot be had for under $300 a month unless you are fortunate enough to have your parent admitted at less than cost to one of the nursing homes or wings or sections affiliated with a voluntary hospital or nonprofit home for the aged.

Many of the children who can well afford nursing home care for their aged parents unwisely hesitate to arrange for it, however, because of the same kind of feelings of guilt against which we have frequently cautioned. There was Mrs. Collins, for instance, who, against her mother's physician's advice, kept the bedfast ninety-two-year old woman living with her. Virtuously she explained why to her friends.

"Of course it would be easier for *me*," she said. "And actually, having to keep and feed help so I'm not absolutely tied down all the time, it would probably cost less. But my maternal grandmother lived with us when I was a girl and *my* mother didn't relegate *her* to be with strangers when she was old. No, Granny died right in her own bed, and the least I can do for Mother is show the same devotion." What Mrs. Collins forgot, or overlooked, was that during the last decade of her life Granny was marooned in her third-floor back bedroom of a New York City brownstone house whose flights of long, steep stairs had become too much for her; that her meals came up in a dumbwaiter and she ate them alone; and that although the youngsters in the family were instructed to go to see Granny at least once a day, their visits were minimal and perfunctory. Also, she did not consider that in her own ranch-type suburban house with the lovely bedroom and bath added at the far end of the patio especially for Mother, Mother, confined to her room, was almost as isolated as Granny had been and perhaps even more poignantly, for she could dimly hear the chatter and laughter of guests without having any more contact with them than polite "How do you do's" and "How are you feeling's?" when they called briefly to pay their respects. Actually an invalided old person rarely or never able to leave his room can feel more achingly "relegated" and out of things in a family home, where he cannot be a real participant in the life of the household, than in a nursing home which revolves around people like himself.

With false sentimentality similar to Mrs. Collins', Jim Haydon deprived his severely arthritic mother of companionship. A corporation employee stationed in Rome, he flew home when he learned that his brothers and sisters, upon medical advice and after a long, thoughtful family huddle, had arranged for Mrs. Haydon to be admitted to an excellent, friendly nursing home with a physical therapist on its staff. "I won't have *my* mother in an institution," he stormed. Old Mrs. Haydon, who had already become a kind of leader in the social life of the place and was contented until his blustering advent, soon let him convince her how forlorn and abused she was, and against the laments of half a dozen old lady and two old gentleman cronies, consented to live with him. Without heeding the pleas of his brothers and sisters or consulting his wife, who had remained abroad, off he bore his mother to live miserably in his home.

The Jim Haydons were childless and the elder Mrs. Haydon yearned for all the grandchildren left behind in the United States. She didn't understand the ways of the Italian servants and they didn't understand hers, which might have been all right had she not been left alone with them so much; young Melinda Haydon led a very active social life. Besides, she and her mother-in-law had never liked each other overmuch so it suited them both to spend as little time together as possible. It wasn't even much better when Jim was home evenings and weekends, there was always so much company, much of it foreigners, with whom she didn't fit. She knew that Roman medicine must be all right, or Rome couldn't have lasted so long, but still she missed her own American doctor and physical therapist. After a year she screwed up the courage to tell Jim that she'd like to go back to the States, and having demonstrated his superior devotion to his brothers and sisters, he consented. Today Mrs. Haydon, back in the nursing home, organizing card games and acting as a kind of greeter to newcomers, is generally as cheerful as her painful physical condition permits.

It may be not you, but your parent, who protests a move to a nursing home. His pleas may tear your heart, but rather than succumb to them, help him adjust to the plan agreed upon after due deliberation by the family, his doctor, and perhaps also a caseworker. Try to get him to understand why this step is necessary or desirable; ask his physician and minister to help him accept the situation. Enlisting a public health nurse might also be helpful, or perhaps there is a social worker or someone else on the staff of the nursing home you have under consideration who is qualified and available to counsel him beforehand. If possible, take your mother or father to see the nursing home and meet the administrator before he or she actually enters it as a patient. Both you and your parent should be satisfied with her personality and the impression of integrity, sincerity, and warmth that she gives. As Ralph Waldo Emerson put it, "Any institution is the length and shadow of a single individual," so whoever heads a nursing home sets its whole tone.

Since the reason that your parent has to go to a nursing home is because he needs constant care, it would be unrealistic for him not to feel largely dependent. But avoid dwelling on this aspect of the situation. The right kind of nursing home will enable him to retain or regain every shred of independence as long as possible, from feeding and dressing himself to doing small chores like straightening up magazines or watering plants that will make him feel useful to others. Above all, be optimistic—with him, and in your own mind. Because inferior "nursing homes"—which are often not nursing homes at all, as we have said—seem like the last downward step to death, too few families realize that the good ones are often a temporary upward stopover with the patient returning to his own home in improved physical health and mental clarity.

It may be wise therefore, to find the best nursing home your parent or you can afford. Even from a hard-boiled financial point of view, a relatively expensive few months, even a year or so, might cost less in the long run than the remainder of a lifetime at low rates. Even if privacy is important to your parent, it might be better for him to be in a two- or three-bed room where there are skilled nursing care and rehabilitative therapies than in a private room at another place too low-priced to afford much more than keeping him alive and relatively comfortable. What's more, some aged patients, no matter how much they want a private room at first, find that they are lonesome after a while and ask to be moved where they have a roommate.

Before you start to look for a nursing home, find out whether there is a referral service specifically for nursing homes in your community, and if not, whether the council of social agencies (which may be called the United Givers Fund or the Health and Welfare Council or have some other name) has a listing of them. The local mental health association may be able to steer you, and in any case, the local health department can provide you with the names of licensed homes although it is unlikely to evaluate them for you. A few states publish directories of nursing homes and other facilities for the aged.

Get professional help on the detailed criteria you should use when you visit nursing homes within your price range. Much of what we have outlined for evaluating homes for the aged (Chapter 8) as to occupation, diversion, accessibility, worship, outings, and community relations applies also to nursing homes. In addition, may we caution you not to let anyone tell you that a nursing home is "bound to smell." With scrupulous cleanliness of both patients and premises, adequate ventilation, the toilet training effective for all but the tiny fraction of aged patients who are incurably incontinent and sufficient employees promptly to change the sheets of that tiny fraction, there is no reason either for any unpleasant stuffy odor nor the covering odor of strong disinfectants. Also, beware of the person who informs you that "with our kind of patients, most have to be in bed." Most should be up, not left lying to deteriorate physically and mentally. It takes work and an adequate number of employees to get old people out of bed, but this is part of good nursing. A majority of bedfast patients are an indication of understaffing; or of staff who find it easier to "know where they are" and to "give them trays" rather than get them up, perhaps under protest, to go to a dining room; or of a shortage of essential equipment like wheel chairs and walkers; or, worse, a dishonest taking advantage of the higher welfare rates paid for bedfast patients.

At best the search for a nursing home is never an easy experience for a concerned son or daughter. Even in superior nursing homes your first sight of a group of feeble, sick, and perhaps befuddled old men and women is liable to come as a shock. "Could *my* mother or father ever get to be like this?" is your natural, unconscious reaction. Return a second time and the impact should be lessened; you will be able to be more objective about the nursing home itself. Also, bear in mind the fact that if your parent is among those more decrepit than he, under wise nursing guidance it might actually set him up, for he may be helped to feel useful to others, as was Mrs. Collins about whom we wrote earlier in this chapter.

Perhaps, in addition to the whole disturbing problem of having your parent in a nursing home, you have geographical tizzies. That is, you may be living in the North while your parent, who years ago retired to the Southwest or Southeast or Far West, has the residential requirements to enter a nonprofit nursing home in one of those areas, or wants to remain where he has later-life friends. But by all means let him stay where he wishes. Bear in mind the fact that nowadays the distance to anywhere by air is measurable by a few hours, not by formidable miles; that long-distance telephone rates at certain hours are minuscule, and that the time is not far off when you will be able to show off the new in-law and new baby with a telephone call!

Once your parent is established in a nursing home, your job is by no means over. It is highly important that you visit, write, continue to show your interest in him. Although any good nursing home works closely with physicians, either through staff consultation, or by close and continued contact with patients' own physicians, it is important that you, too, make sure that your parent have periodic medical and dental care. It is also part of your continuing job to get a psychiatric evaluation if he manifests increased confusion as to where and when, or has emotional difficulties, or undergoes a change in personality. Theoretically a good nursing home should assume this responsibility, but things as they are are not always as they should be, so by taking it on as your own you may either save your parent from deteriorating mentally and emotionally or remove him in time to where he can get needed, intensive psychiatric care.

Pay attention to your parent's complaints and report them to the proper authority, but be careful not to let any guilt feelings of your own make you unduly carping and picky. Often old people play on their children's sympathy and work up an unjustified case against a person or institution in order to make a son or daughter feel remorseful about having put them where they are. Also, your aged parent may be confused and mistake a treatment for cruelty, a diet as deprivation.

Visit as often as the rules—which should be liberal—permit. If he is able to go out, have him visit you. Write chatty letters about family and neighborhood doings which will help your parent feel that ties with the outside world are not entirely severed. Remember holidays and birthdays with gifts, for little attentions take on a large and heartwarming significance to the old. Don't become discouraged and stop giving if the bed jacket you spent a good deal of time making or the fine handbag or tobacco pouch on which you spread yourself—perhaps at the sacrifice of your doing without a new one yourself—are never used but put into a bureau drawer in their original wrappings. A gift given for love is cherished with love, you may be sure, and the very reason it is not used is likely to be because your parent holds it so dear and precious. Maintain all such contacts no matter how indifferent your parent may seem, for no one can ever tell what might trickle into the consciousness of even the most apparently inert bodies or confused minds. No matter what happens, or where your parent is, you need not and should not ever abdicate as a child.

The whole job of children's carrying out their responsibilities toward aging parents, with all its implications, is summed up in a simple Mexican legend. Juan, so it goes, no longer wanted to be burdened with his father, who had become feeble and useless. So he told his son to conduct the old man to a remote mountainside. "But be sure to leave with him a little food and a blanket, so that he will have some comfort," Juan said. When the boy returned, he was carrying half a blanket.

"Why do you bring back half the blanket?" Juan demanded.

The boy said, "I am saving it for you."

EPILOGUE

YOU AND THE COMMUNITY

YOUR PARENTS ARE not the only elderly people with whom you need to be concerned. About half of all Americans sixty-five and over are too poor to afford a decent place to live, proper food, adequate medical care, or essential recreation. Typically they mark time until death in tumbledown rural shacks; shabby, unsafe, unsanitary furnished rooms in decayed urban neighborhoods; or in fetid "nursing homes" which, like the Holy Roman Empire that was neither Holy nor Roman nor an empire, afford neither nursing care nor a homelike atmosphere. Many, if not most, unlike your parents, have no children to be concerned about them, either because they are childless or have survived their descendants. Some have dropped below the poverty line from the middle class because of later-life unemployment or expensive, prolonged illness. The majority have been poor all their lives, which means that from birth they have lacked adequate nutrition and medical care and that their sicknesses in old age are disastrously compounded. Against the backdrop of our affluent society, our ailing, impoverished, isolated, and desperately lonely aged do not make a pretty picture.

Too many of us delude ourselves that "welfare" or social security or sweet charity take care of all the needs of the aged, and that they can always get free medical care at an outpatient clinic or in a hospital bed. As well-authenticated testimony at Senate hearings has evidenced, this simply isn't so.

As this book goes to press, the medicare issue is hot and controversial and we shall not attempt to go into it. We do, however, want to give a few suggestions as to how you might help better the lot of old people less fortunate than the parent who has you as a child.

Provision of more and better nursing homes is crucial, for as matters stand, nursing home economics cannot work out. In these United States, the care of the sick aged is a business. Nine out of ten nursing homes are "proprietary"—that is, privately owned and run for profit. Like any other American business, the nursing home business is competitive, and therefore the more a nursing home gives for the money the more beds it is likely to have filled. This is fine for those who can more than pay their way. But as we said in Chapter 27, actual cost of nursing-home care is a minimum of $300 a month. With public assistance payments for nursing-home care ranging from $50 a month in the lowest-paying state to a little over $200 in the highest, figure out for yourself what a patient can get when someone has to make even a modest profit. There is a crying need for non-profit nursing-home beds. Through your church or local hospital, work for having it filled.

Community preventive measures can keep many an old person from having to have residential care. For years, at the ridiculously low cost of a few cents per month per patient, Philadelphia's outpatient mental health clinic has kept old people from needing to go to mental hospitals. In New York City, from the Hodson Center, where impecunious, lonely old folks living in furnished rooms find recreation, activity, friends, and participation in a kind of community of their own, not a single man or woman has descended into residential dependence.

Help to organize homemaker service in your community (see Chapter 3) and you will also help its aged to live more happily and independently. Sponsorship of a recreation or crafts center may bridge the gap between nothingness and misery and a life worth living for the old. Urge and encourage your local government or privately supported agency to establish a system of foster-home care, through which aged men and women without families of their own or even with families of their own (see Chapter 7) may experience the warm joys of integration in family life. Sometimes welfare checks are sufficient for the old people to pay their own way in family homes, so it may take only prodding from you to get such service inaugurated with little or no extra cost to taxpayers.

Relatively new and still incompletely defined on the old-age scene are *Protective Services for Older Persons* (for sale by the Superintendent of Documents, U.S. Government Printing Office, Washington, D.C. 20402; price 20 cents). What they mainly add up to is financial and legal help and advice for older clients unable to look after their own affairs. Strengthen and support the Legal Aid Society in your community and you help to keep off crooked and exploiting lawyers who prey upon those helpless and defenseless like the old.

Even the inauguration of a telephone checking service (see Chapter 3) may stave off unhappy dependence, not only for your own parents, but also for other less fortunate aged members of your community. Quite shockingly, some five million of the aged poor do not have in their homes the telephone contact which is elementary in the rest of technological America.

Support federal measures that assist your state to develop programs of housing and services for the aged. On a more immediate level, serve as a volunteer in any place where the aged may need warm, kindly, personal interest. (See Chapter 20.) In doing this, you may get an unanticipated dividend. As parents of young children who see other young children in groups come to be rather pleased with their own, because they acquire standards based on reality rather than their own wishful thinking, so will you tend to be less critical or less overprotective of your aging parents if you become better acquainted with their contemporaries.

And if you have lost your parents, what better memorial can you give them than your dedication to the cause of other old people?

INDEX